BEYOND
THE
NOW

REVIEWS & ENDORSEMENTS
FOR JASON SHULMAN'S WORK

About The Instruction Manual for Receiving God:

"A Dharma teacher and Kabbalist, Jason Shulman has succeeded in creating a down-to-earth guide which makes the quest to find God into a realizable possibility."

> — Deepak Chopra, M.D., author of Life After Death:
> The Burden of Proof

"Beautiful lessons and brilliant insights on the divine nature of humanity and how we connect with God and ourselves. Enlightening and inspirational."

> — Stephen R. Covey, author, *The 7 Habits of Highly
> Effective People* and *The 8th Habit: From Effectiveness to
> Greatness*

"The Instruction Manual for Receiving God contains exactly the type of common-sense wisdom required for a person to live a good old-fashioned grounded life in a society that encourages us to do things faster while multi-tasking. This book is a magnificent breath of tranquil air."

> — Caroline Myss, author of *Anatomy of the Spirit* and
> *Sacred Contracts*

"Jason Shulman offers us a profoundly simple guide to the obviousness of awakening to our deepest Self. Lucid, contemporary, and most of all kind, this is a beautiful book which goes to the very heart of the human condition, by encouraging us to embrace both the impersonal oneness of all things and the richness of the personal life."

> — Timothy Freke, author of *Lucid Living*

"A beautiful book that brings the western spiritual tradition into our modern world. It's deep, thoughtful, exciting, and we can use it to find out how we live when we are fully human."

— John Tarrant, author of *Bring Me the Rhinoceros*

About Kabbalistic Healing: A Path to an Awakened Soul:

"Jason Shulman is a true adept of the inner teachings. He offers a very sophisticated and dynamic account of what happens between the Kabbalah and the great, luminous transparency. To engage with Jason Shulman's mind is to enter into the reality where true healing can occur."

— Rabbi Zalman Schachter-Shalomi, Founder of the Jewish Renewal Movement

"This lucid book of deep healing is a brilliant contribution to the spiritual literature bridging Eastern and Western thought. Shulman's bigger view unifies seeking and being-there, path and goal, transcendence and immanence, with the joy of a true master."

— Lama Surya Das, founder of the Dzogchen Center and author of *Awakening the Buddha Within*

"Jason Shulman brilliantly integrates a deep psychological component with a profound understanding of the non-dual, absolute unity of the Divine Nature in a way that raises the reader's soul to the highest potential of awareness. While traditional teachings tend to demean the ego-self, Shulman shows us the importance of our gift of self-awareness and how to come to peace with ourselves. Thus he leads readers to evoke a healing from our sense of fractured separation into a wholeness of being that has compassion for who we are and what we are. This is a must-read for anyone who wishes to learn the essence of kabbalistic teachings in the hands of a master of spiritual and psychological development."

— Rabbi David A. Cooper, author of *God Is a Verb*

"Here is once and future wisdom as we meet the Jewish mystical tradition in its revelatory mapping of the nature of reality. Here too are practices that bring the reader closer to the nondual state of consciousness and awareness of the integral relationship between all things. Taken seriously, this profound work can only charge the spirit as it illumines the mind and heart."

— Jean Houston, PH.D., author of *Jump Time: Shaping Your Future in a World of Radical Change*

"Kabbalistic Healing is a great book about discovering wisdom within each of us. At a time when everyone in contemporary society is experiencing an information glut, what's missing is a deeper understanding of life. Jason Shulman provides the reader with wisdom and insight for life's journey."

— Stephan Rechtschaffen, cofounder of the Omega Institute for Holistic Studies, and creator and director of Blue Spirit Costa Rica.

"Jason Shulman is a sincere, authentic practitioner of Kabbalah. The fruit of much inner work, the masterful teachings in this book resonate and come alive because he has truly experienced this wisdom from deep inside."

— Rabbi Tirzah Firestone, author of *The Receiving: Reclaiming Jewish Women's Wisdom* and *With Roots in Heaven*

OTHER WORKS BY JASON SHULMAN

Re-breathing Buddha's Four Noble Truths

The Nondual Shaman™: A Contemporary Shamanistic Path & Thoroughgoing Training for Awakening the Self

The Kabbalah Monographs:
> The Work of Briah
> [The Set of the World]
> The Master of Hiddenness
> The Configurations

Ecstatic Speech: Expressions of True Nonduality

The MAGI Process: A Nondual Method for Personal Awakening and the Resolution of Conflict

What does reward bring you but to bind you to Heaven like a slave? (Poetry)

The Instruction Manual for Receiving God

Kabbalistic Healing: A Path to an Awakened Soul

BEYOND THE NOW

ESSAYS ON
THE HEART
OF ENLIGHTENMENT

JASON SHULMAN

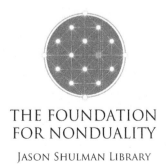

THE FOUNDATION
FOR NONDUALITY

JASON SHULMAN LIBRARY

The Foundation for Nonduality
Oldwick, New Jersey 08833

Series Editor: Nancy Yielding
Series Managing Editor: Kimberly Burnham
Editorial Counselor: Shelah Stein
Cover and Interior Design: Tom Schneider
MS Word mise-en-scène: Jeff Casper

FIRST EDITION 2021

ISBN: 978-0-9972201-5-5

10 9 8 7 6 5 4 3 2 1

DEDICATION

To my beloved, who taught me that the real miracle is
that there is anything here at all.

TABLE OF CONTENTS

FOREWORD

Blessings. Jason Shulman is a blessing—that's what his heart, his soul and his teachings are made of. I am not saying that he is pure and has risen above the challenges of being a human being. In fact, he is a man who has traversed many sacred lands as well as arid wastelands as he delved into transmuting the wounds of his history. He is devoted to healing and teaching the truth of the dharma as he lives an "ordinary" life with family.

Jason is a tertön, a Tibetan term that means he is a person who is a discoverer of ancient hidden texts or terma. He has unearthed ancient, hidden and indescribably loving paths and practices to awakening, true intimacy, quality, true presence, and seismic-shifting soul retrieval. These teachings are profoundly exquisite because they include all of the human conditions. Nothing, absolutely nothing is left out. From here, an alchemical return into our heart of hearts creates an everlasting activation of our deepest longing—to be the totality of who we are, who we were born to be, our

1

truest and most original self. Jason's teachings are for all of us who want to wake up and live fully. Through his work we learn how to walk the walk of awakening and healing in a soul-touching and practical way. Twenty-four years ago, I attended a "Kabbalah and Ecstasy" workshop with Jason at a workshop at the Omega Institute for Holistic Studies in Rhinebeck, New York. There were over 100 people in that workshop, all of us longing to find our way home to our truest selves. At that time, I was in my early forties. I had a beautiful family and a successful gestalt psychotherapy practice on Long Island, New York. I was a Reiki master, a meditation teacher and I incorporated other types of energy work into my practice. Even with all of the psychotherapy, meditation and spiritual practices that I had engaged with for over twenty years at that point, something was missing. I knew there was more, I could feel it, I could smell it, it was magnetic, and it would talk to me. People once said, and maybe they still do, when you are ready the teacher will appear. That was hard for me to appreciate and take in. I thought I had been ready for a long time; I had been questing for so long. I prayed to meet my teacher. In that first workshop, I opened to the realization that being an imperfect human being, living an ordinary life was a great starting point. And honestly, I was shocked to learn that merging into the oneness of the great unknown was not the answer. Maybe just maybe, I could actually be myself. I didn't even know exactly what that meant.

Most importantly, Jason has worked deeply and continuously on himself, unfolding more and more of his healing and awakening. He teaches how to truly own what it is like to be an imperfect "foolish being" who falls down and gets back up over and over again. But he is so much more. He is a brilliant spiritually infused man who has committed himself to constant practice, self-honesty and compassion. As a teacher he is deeply serious and deeply funny. I can't tell you how often we have laughed in our classes and personal conversations together. And his music is a delight that transports us into a state of wholeness, a home deep into our heart of hearts.

This book is a compilation of essays on nonduality. But they are more than that, each one is a transmission. Each sentence is the thing itself and shares with us the fundamental pivot into our greatest joy-coming home. The title of this book, Beyond the Now, expresses Jason's understanding that the so called "now" is not the final resting place in our spiritual search. It is, of course, an important experience to have on our spiritual journey, but true nonduality does not stop there.

As Jason says:

...the now is often confused with what enlightenment or the awakened state is like. Beneath this approach, of trying to

find transcendental oneness and reject the relative, are some basic misconceptions about the spiritual path which ultimately lead to deep spiritual problems. The major problem is that in our effort to gain this magical state of enlightenment, we split the world into two parts: the part we think is spiritual and the part we think is simply pain. The part we want to avoid and the part we want to go after. So, based on this thinking, we go after what we think enlightenment is made of. True enlightenment, on the other hand, refuses to split the world into "pure" and "impure," or the "absolute" and the "relative."

In these essays Jason shows us again and again how the one and the many are forever joined in the act of creation. Existence implies that oneness and separateness are a single thing, co-arising and co-dependent. Our ego is not our enemy but our vehicle to wholeness. Our individuality and separateness are equally as important as our abiding oneness with everything. In these twenty-six short essays, Jason transmits not only an understanding of the nature of reality but a clear path to how we can live an "enlightening" life as the mysterious, complex, foolish human beings we are. As such, we learn from these teachings how to live in a true state of compassion for others, the world and, most importantly, for our imperfect human selves.

My prayer for all of you, is that you experience the deep blessing in each of these essays.

Eileen Marder Mirman

PREFACE

The majority of these essays were written in the years between 2000 and 2012. They represent the ongoing conversation between me and reality, as I tried to come to an understanding about the deeply nondual nature of us both. They formed, essentially, the philosophical background to the foreground creation of Nondual Kabbalistic Healing, Impersonal Movement, The Work of Return and the Magi Process, all practical ways of putting into action a new understanding of what nonduality is and how it affects all our actions, thoughts, feelings and relationships.

We are all here only for a while. At its best, our time is spent in a sort of melancholy dance of joy, the bittersweet journey of time-bound beings who have eternity on their minds. Nonduality—when rightly seen—offers us a path not so much out of this dilemma, but one that evokes our inner dignity so that we learn to meet each challenge not as a pauper but as a millionaire, a person rich in the ways of time, earth, sky and water; a person for whom relationship, reified and rectified, becomes the unfolding of all things good.

To that end, each of these essays, while emanating from my own questions, seeks to clarify the concept of nonduality since there is a lot of misinformation going around regarding this topic. This misinformation has the consequence of pushing the very freedom we are seeking further away, splitting the world into an acceptable "spiritual" part and a part that needs to be discarded. This is, of course, not true. All of reality is holy and awakening to this truth helps heal those parts that have been injured so that they can gather together again as the totality of our being, a being who is at once separate and unique and simultaneously part of an undividable whole.

My greatest desire is that these works help you, that you feel freer and more accepting of yourself after reading them, that you begin to have faith in yourself as an imperfect Buddha, a devotee of the truth. Above all, I hope that through some of these essays I can share with you new ways to be kind to yourself. Learning kindness toward myself has been the greatest gift I've received. It is kindness toward ourselves that—at the beginning—gives us the emotional and spiritual room to start working directly with our suffering. And it is kindness again, this time toward all of creation, that seems to be the goal of all spiritual learning.

I hope we can all become builders of bridges. First between the disparate parts of ourselves and, eventually, between ourselves and other people. Spiritual work is the work of locating yourself as you are, knowing that you are a perfect being who still needs healing. As we heal, we become more firmly located in our own lives and because of that, shine more brightly in our lives as they are. And being who we are in this way, we bring more unity to the world around us, one little bit at a time. That seems to me to be a fine thing.

Jason Shulman

FIRST LIGHT

Calling to Light

I remember, as a child of three or so, crouching in the garden of the brownstone we shared with my grandparents and my aunt and uncle, and talking to a small white butterfly. I actually remember that some of the things I said had to do with wondering what life was about. I wondered who the butterfly was and who I was. I wondered if we could communicate. I wondered where we go when we are no longer here. It was a defining moment for me—a call from the world to some place deep in my soul—and it has never left me. Though it was a conversation of questions, I understand now that it was also a moment of companionship with the world, a feeling of oneness and duality at the same moment.

Most of us have had these childhood moments of revelation and often long for them throughout the rest of our life. We sometimes think they will never come again. But we can help ourselves return to these moments of wholeness anew if we learn to listen to the great calling that we are made of, that we are: the calling of ourselves to our self, which is the essence of our life.

If we allow ourselves to be quiet and put aside all the voices in our head for a few moments, we can become aware of a sort of pressure to move forward, to find the truth, to know what is right, to solve the mystery. We feel an urge in ourselves, in our bodies or minds or feelings, that makes us seek something. We could say—if we let ourselves dream a bit—that we are being called by something, something inside us or even outside us. If we think about this in this way, we could say that every one of you reading this is called. We are all wondering how to live a better life, a life that is filled with a sense of really living. We are called to life.

We may think that we have come to this moment of our lives out of curiosity or by accident. But my understanding is that we are all here because we are called by something or someone or some force that seems to guide our lives.

Even when we feel we are *not* called, we feel sorrow because somewhere in us we remember what it is like to be called or connected to this something, even if we have never consciously admitted this thought to ourselves or actually heard this calling. In this case, the longing or sorrow *is* the calling itself in another form.

For many years, I taught that much of this pressure was created by the ego's relentless quest to control life. From that perspective, this pressure was a way to escape the now into some favored future or past. I continue to believe in the truth of this, but—as I've learned to see duality as it is and become more aware of the holiness of this realm of duality and opposites—I also see more clearly than ever that there is another calling going on that does not arise from the ego. And yet, it simultaneously does arise from it since the healing ego is an instrument that is dedicated not only to survival but to change and awakening. I have come to see that this calling to the ego eventually becomes its crowning glory and achievement.

However, when we first begin thinking about the nature of this "calling" we can easily experience confusion: Does this calling exist, and if it does, what exactly is it? Why should there even be a call? Is it a figment of our imagination? Wishful thinking? The desperate hope of someone who is lost? Some illusion that we made up that needs to be cleared away? Is there a person or a god calling us? The thought is at once thrilling and terrifying; it also has the power to raise the skeptic in us to great prominence. When we begin to think about this calling, doubt becomes king.

We all start out in these early stages of doubt. But I have seen time and again that, as we continue our journey, we go through three spiritual developmental stages that eventually bring us to understand that separateness and oneness can unite, and that the caller and the call are one.

The First Stage of Being Called

We might call the first stage the stage of overpowering *static* or *noise*. In this stage, we cannot hear the calling because our ears are filled with the sounds of our history. These sounds—the noise of imperfect upbringing, childhood pain and terror, miseducation by accident or design, religious misconception, human limitation and fear—block out our true nature, which is to hear this calling to our souls.

We are being taught by this noise—which is information of a sort, perpetuated by our families and culture—how not to be ourselves but to live in the story of our history or the story of our rebellion against our history, both of which are unsatisfactory solutions to the puzzle of being real.

It is only when the pain of our existence gets loud enough and we have failed to find enduring happiness, that we begin the journey of clearing away this noise, of separating the music of life from the voices of those who would deny us this authenticity and the parts of ourselves that would deny us this as well. This leads us to the second stage of being called.

The Second Stage of Being Called

We might name this the stage of surrounding ourselves with our own sound. In this stage, we begin to notice that *we* like certain things and *do not* like other things. We find the world of *preference* and simultaneously find we have the power to make changes in our lives. We find the power to choose. We no longer simply have to react to life but can direct it as well.

Since all of our development as human beings is uneven, in certain arenas we excel in seeking out what we long for while in other areas we remain trapped, still shackled by historical wounds.

As we progress in this stage however, we find more areas in our lives where we can seek out the things we long for. It takes long and sometimes arduous work to have the faith to continue our journey. We meet with our own and the world's resistance to change and happiness, even as we all claim to want nothing but happiness.

Simultaneous to the resistance, however, in this stage we begin to notice how the world itself seems to present opportunities to lead us inward to deeper and deeper paths.

Because of the holographic nature of the world—which sometimes shows itself as synchronicity, accident, hunches and intuitions—the world begins to show its cooperation, offering ways pleasant and unpleasant, into the inner chambers of our being.

At first it is mystical: we put in the work and something comes back. We don't understand the causality. It seems like magic. Eventually though, we begin to trust this new arrangement. As Christ said: "Knock and the door shall be opened." We find this to be true.

It is during this stage that we begin to hear the call more clearly, though even now we may not call it "a calling." But more and more, we find ourselves with people of like mind and thought; we seek out situations that will challenge us and teach us, and we feel increasingly glad to learn.

When that openness has settled into our bodies and minds, when we begin to trust it, we realize this call to our soul is happening all the time. There is something in us that wants to know the truth and will do anything to seek it out. It does not stop for day or night, good weather or bad. It has a single clarion call that sounds its tone beneath everything we do. However, in the beginning of this realization, *seeking* is often used by the ego to prove its point of *never being good enough,* or *never having gone far enough to be completely safe.* We are still caught in an unhealed, egoic drama.

We only begin to understand little by little that even this remnant of the egoic dilemma serves the greater purpose of inexorably bringing us to our goal of being with God or reality or authenticity. The hint of this truth—that no matter what we do we are always moving forward—brings us to the beginning of the third stage of hearing the call.

The Third Stage of Being Called

The third stage begins when we start to realize *we have no choice*. What does this mean? The baseball player has no choice but to play, the singer to sing, the painter to paint. Now, after having gone through the stage of not even being able to hear our own heart, we start to hear it and vow to never give it up.

Even if we forget our vow for a while, even for a long while, we always try to find a way to return to ourselves, to return to our own heart. We see that we have no choice but to listen. And we are glad for this. We do not feel controlled or limited by this almost instinctive voice that survives in us; rather, we feel blessed, because we are doing what we were meant to do.

Forgetting this truth and remembering it, over and over again (for it is our nature to find our way and lose it over and over again), we one day have the realization that *this calling is inside of us as well as outside of us.* It is then that we begin to realize the true meaning of this call. Then the secrets of this calling are revealed, even as they become more mysterious than ever.

We begin to understand that this call to the spirit is not something extra, something that comes out of the mouth of some being or god who is standing to the side and calling to us, but that this calling itself *is* God, or Buddha's voice, or truth itself, and that this calling is where our personal heart and the heart of the universe coincide and become congruent.

We understand this because of a profound change in attitude that takes place when we practice *listening:* when our history is healed enough that we can hear the call that comes from the world, we also realize that we are forever calling within ourselves; then we find that even the unhealed ego within us calls. Powerfully but sweetly, our most personal self asks us to seek reality, or Buddha, or any guiding principle or entity to find the truth; it is the very nature of our personal self to *call to the one who calls.*

Often what we take for our "personal self" is really a conglomerate of defenses, responses, and reactions to our history. As these conglomerates are understood, the personal self begins to soften. Edges that once were brittle and cold become warmer and more enveloping. Boundaries that were once too weak to solidly contain the energy of life become solid in a healthy way and able to sustain the ups and downs of life's movements without shattering or losing faith.

It is then we see that our personal self is made of this calling; that its nature is to call, to attract, to hold, to love and *be* compassion. We have a hint of a great truth: the personal self does not *express* compassion; it *is* compassion. And when we hear the call within long enough, we turn our consciousness away from the content (indicating that there is something "out there" to find) to the essence of it. We find we are made of the desire of God Itself to see all of Creation. The very will to constantly search for God *is* God. Nothing else need be found or done. The quest ends with the recognition of what the essence of the seeker has been all along: Love itself. We are all born to be *bodhisattvas*—or helpers of humankind and all of creation—if we only let it happen.

We ourselves are this very call. We are calling to ourselves. We are, so to speak, in two places at once, inside and outside, listening and speaking. We are made of this calling and are walking in the dimension of this calling. We begin to consider that the universe doesn't *contain* this calling but is *made* of this calling, because it seems to be everywhere we look. Heaven and Earth are one. Considering and feeling these truths, we look at the world and ourselves in a new way. We no longer feel so separate from the world and no longer feel so alienated from ourselves. There is something that connects the dual and separate to the great oneness. Life itself becomes the manifestation of this truth; its finest expression.

It becomes our job then—our holy work—to constantly do the work that lets the personal self become free of its history so that it can soften and strengthen enough to hear, first, the call from the outer universe and then, second, to hear the call from the universe within, until there is no difference.

This is not making the world over in our own neurotic image. It is letting go of images entirely. This journey does not dissolve the personal self. It actually elevates the personal self to its rightful place: the *expression* or *manifestation* of God's real singularity and accordance with duality. In *A Society of Souls,* our school of healing and spiritual work, we call this rectified self the *personal with no history.*

Only the healing personality can have a personal relationship with all, with God, with the *atman* (personal life principle), with *brahma* (self-born creative spirit), with the *Ayn-Sof* (infinite without end), and this personal relationship is not mysterious or distant. The path within this third stage consists simply of continuing the effort to be ourselves.

Because of the nature of the universe, this *being ourselves* can only be found by a combination of effort and allowing. Because the nature of the wounded ego——educated by imperfect parents and an imperfect society——is to never be satisfied, and to always be looking for the next world to conquer, the act of allowing ourselves *to be as we are*, is an enormously courageous one. It is the enemy of pride and fear and a friend to our inner longing to see our rightful place in heaven and earth. At the same time, we must make constant effort to release the ego from the accrued debris of lifetimes of overlays laid down by this same faulty development. All the effort we put out must be done with exquisite kindness. Without that, it is only a type of effort that *opposes* being. *With* kindness however, this effort is a manifestation of who we truly are, and thus does not violate our true nature.

We might say it is living a life of worship——the personal worship of constant effort. We put out effort so that the "great allowing" we call "God," can manifest within the separate being we seem to be. Effort freely given in this way is the life of true nondualism, its worshipful gaze not beholden to any superstition or learned thing but supported by a deep and abiding sense of the real. It takes skill to know when to allow and when to work. Only when both of these acts are faithfully accomplished can we return to what we might call *the first light,* that initial and constant glow or hum in the center of our being.

The nature of light is that there must be a source and an object that this light falls upon, something separate to be illuminated. Through our efforts to free ourselves from the chains of the past and our simultaneous letting ourselves be, we find that we are the object that is illuminated and, surprisingly, also the light itself. Knowing this, we see that our separate existence *is* this *first light.* We are illuminated as we are.

The state of *first light* overthrows all convention. It speaks and it is silent. It is the sound of the *aleph* without a vowel; it is the Tibetan seed-syllable "Ah!" Sometimes it is called *love,* but this is the love that is beyond feeling and not feeling. It is a state of existence; it is existence itself. When our eyes and ears are open, we get to actually see and hear this around us, in all of creation.

Return to Light

In the third stage we begin to realize that this call goes out to everyone equally; the very nature of the call is its very evenness, its universality. It is in every location and not limited to a special place or time. This has the effect of allowing our separateness *and* our oneness to exist simultaneously. This is the condition that is necessary for our awareness of our connection to the *first light*.

The story of Jesus can be illuminating here. Whether this is a path we have chosen or not makes no difference. Jesus was known religiously as "the son of God." This phrase can also be misleading if we do not understand the third stage, the stage in which—now being free from the overt demands of the wounded ego—we begin to feel the pulse of the "great mother," the "great luminous silence of *what-is*". If we think about the phrase "son of God" literally, we realize that this is a description of family: the son of God means the progeny, the offspring of God. Christ is known as the first son because he has realized something *first-hand* that is more fundamental than being the second or third son. Translating this we can say that *first-hand* is direct knowledge of the real—that is, the combined insight of the personal and the transcendent, while second or third-hand knowledge only *points* to the real. Of course, any son or daughter, first, second or third, can have first-hand knowledge.

What these words are saying to me is that in order for us—that is *all of us*—to have first-hand knowledge, we must understand that there is something that is calling to us *personally*, and that the outcome of hearing this call deeply enough within our own soul is to discover that we do not "own" this calling, that in fact, it is not only directed toward every manifest thing, but that the act of existence itself *is this calling*. Listening and calling are same thing from this perspective. Just as water was born to *flow*, we are born both to listen and to call to our greater Self. From this perspective, the entire spiritual path is the return to understanding that we are all the first sons and daughters; each one of us is an "only child!" in a universe of children.

This is what Jesus knew himself to be, and he knew not only that, but that everyone and everything in the universe has as its essence, in its core, this simple thing, that is personal and not personal at the same time, an eddy in a river but not the river, a river with eddy that defines and beautifies the river.

The call the universe makes to us is to be ourselves completely. This call encourages us to work as hard as we can to be empty enough of obstacles so that the calling itself can be heard in all its thrilling notes. There is nothing beyond this, no deeper truth, no special content in this calling that is the secret message. Illumination calls us when we are who we are, just as we are, and we must work with kindness to return to that. This work is not so much to improve ourselves as to *realize ourselves*. To *see ourselves clearly*. When we are consciously, *personally* aware of who we are, flaws and all, greatness and all, we hear God calling.

Knowing who you are is not a mystical thing, but a matter of experience, acceptance, honesty, compassion, and caring. It is knowing you are small and selfish and greedy and angry, and great, creative, tender-hearted, and caring. Sometimes it is the very acknowledgment—paradoxically enough—that you cannot hear the call because you are closed in some way.

When we know about ourselves in this way—without even attempting to change—we know we are connected, Buddha-in-action, the Divine in manifest form, a co-arising separateness with the oneness of it all. As we understand these things, neurotic separateness begins to fall away. We cannot be separate in the crazy, anxious way we are when we are lost. We are found when we have begun to honestly see ourselves, when we know we are essentially the *first son* or *daughter*. We then understand that "first son" is not a rank to be enjoyed by the ego, but a definition of a family relationship, to the extent that it is the state of relationship we might call *primary manifestation*, beyond history: essential, plain, and simple in its nature.

Jesus was a person who knew that beyond his culture, his parents, his time, he was the way God manifests. He walked around with God's calling in his ears. We give this level of knowledge the name "Christ," and it means "to be anointed." Jesus was not afraid to be small, to be fearful, to be lost, to be angry, to be joyful, to be filled with sorrow and gratitude. He was also not afraid—eventually—to be anointed, in the same way we must all be anointed with the tender spirit of our own lives.

To the extent that we can accept our troubled history with love and tenderness (which takes effort of course!), our connection to the unified state is not impeded. Then we begin to understand that God is not far away but is present in our hearts as we reach to find the origin of the call. We need only embrace ourselves in conscious awareness and deep knowledge and reduce our own self-judgements to feel the presence of the Divine. When Jesus says the word "me," as in "the way to the Father is through me," he is really redefining the concept of "me." He is saying *me* is the one who has returned from exile, wounds intact perhaps, but who now knows what the *first light* feels like, who knows his true nature *as* this light. This person is the one who can trust what is beyond the personal self as well. Christ is a description then of the process of return, the anointing of a level of conscious awareness, an awakened affirmation of the fact that we are purely and only manifestations of God, personal waves on the sea of the infinite.

Reaching this level, we *could*—if we desired—say that all of life is impersonal: that is a true picture. After all, the level of the first light cannot be owned. It is to some extent the relinquishing of a personal attitude. The individual self—when its story is believed as the *only* truth—is a distraction from the real unity and thus, the beginning of neurosis itself. But the personal self, accepted as the first light, is beauty itself, a piece of God-manifestation, sparkling in its temporary, effulgent and newly existent self. By being truly who we are, we become undefended. Becoming undefended, we give up the territory. Giving up the territory, we have nothing to reflect upon. With nothing to reflect upon we become empty of preconception and prejudice and open to the way of all ways. Yet, being that way, we also see that we are human and can never give up these things entirely. It is then we hear the call: *Come as you are!* Returning to this state of innocence through the honesty of our search, we can enter a pure land that is right here and right now. We can be as we are: filled with flaws and made of love itself. Personal and impersonal, great and small, wounded and healed, partaking of life and its difficulties, but no longer at the mercy of the opposites of this world.

It is this combination that is our greatness. We make the journey that is impossible to make, we fail and fall into the arms of God. We all always have this chance to shine and, in this shining, fall into our own future, the future when God's face is as easy to see as the back of our hand.

THE NOVEL OF LIFE

When you read a novel and you read about various characters in the novel, you may like some of them and not like others. Or, when you watch a movie, you might think about your relationship with the characters. You might like them; you might not like them. But one thing we can say is that you are not finding your sense of self, your own self, in them. You're not referencing your self-worth by the characters in the novel or when you turn on the TV. You just have your thoughts about them.

But imagine if you turned on your TV or you read a novel and you actually and completely derived your sense of being, your sense of self from one of the characters. Immediately your perspective is going to be very different, right? Now your perspective has gone from something that's very vast to something that's very limited, something seen only through the eyes of the character. Sadly, that's how most human beings spend their lives. They have this little character in their mind called "me," and they're actually viewing that "me" as *personal* when it's not.

The "me" is very impersonal, not meaning cold or distant, but just meaning *without inherent self-nature,* in the same way that when you read a book the characters are without self-nature. They don't actually exist outside of your imagination. They don't even exist in the book, because the book is just words. And without someone reading the words and bringing it all alive within an imaginal space, nothing even exists on the printed page. All this life, all this drama, is actually all within the reader.

When the Buddha talked about the realization of *no-self,* he was talking about the self that is an image in the mind being completely *seen through.* And when there is no image of self there, experience has nothing to bounce off of. Everything just is as it is because there's no secondary interpretation. That moment is the moment we stop listening to the echo and start listening directly to the sound.

It is important to understand that the one who is interpreting—which is to say constantly comparing—is the one who is living in the echo, that's the *who-is* who is in pain. That's the one who suffers. And that's the one who causes others to suffer.

The *image-self,* the self that's an image in the mind, uses every experience to measure itself against something else. "How am I in relationship to what's happening? Am I wise enough? Am I stupid? Am I clumsy? Am I courageous? Am I enlightened enough?" That's the movement of consciousness reflecting on an image of itself that doesn't actually exist. It's always measuring each and every experience and then believing in the interpretation of the experience rather than seeing *"Everything just is…"* Everything actually just is. From the perspective of consciousness, even resistance *just is.* And if you "resist resistance," that's *just what is,* too. You can't get away from it. You start to see that the only thing that goes into resistance to what is, or into a story about or an interpretation of what is—any of these—is this mind-created persona. It's like a character in a novel. When you read a novel, every character has a point of view. It has beliefs. It has opinions. There's something that makes it distinct from other characters. Our persona is literally this mind-created character that's always making itself distinct from everything else. So, it always needs to evaluate everything against its own preconceived ideas.

There is another vantage point, however. The other vantage point is not only outside the character, that is, *seeing the character-ness of the character,* it's also *inside* the character, that is, experiencing the world the way the character sees it. It's the ultimate vantage point, experiencing both positions and not rejecting either one. In this position, we have compassion and sympathy for the character, but we also see it *is* a character in the same moment.

That's basically what it means to really wake up: *we're waking up from the character.* You don't have to destroy the character called "me" to wake up from it. In fact, trying to destroy the character makes it very hard to wake up. Because who is trying to destroy the character? *The character!* What's judging the character? *The character!*

So, leave the character alone. The character called you? Just leave it alone. Then it's much easier for the awakening out of that limited perspective to happen.

When you do this, you don't lose the character; you just gain the whole novel of life. It's not like you lose anything. You just gain the whole book. You gain the whole universe. As Buddha might have said, *lose yourself, gain the universe.* It's not a bad deal. Or Dogen: *To know yourself is to forget yourself and to forget yourself is to be enlightened by the 10,000 things,* which means to see yourself everywhere.

When you wake up from your character you see your self-nature in all characters—not just the one you think you happen to be. You see yourself in all of them. So, we don't lose anything. Instead, we gain all the characters. We just soften our fixation, that's all.

ANY PORT IN A STORM

While a passenger on a cruise trip, experiencing a storm at sea, wants to make port in only a special place—their destination, the place they have paid their money to arrive at—an experienced sailor will tell you: any port in a storm. An experienced sailor looks at the shore differently from someone sailing with a particular destination in mind. To the experienced sailor, every nook and cranny, small inlet or harbor, offers the possibility of safety for boat and crew.

From a certain perspective, we must admit that life is like a storm. Some people have peaceful beginnings: the air and sea are calm; the ocean seems endless and beneficent. Other people are born into different circumstances: they arrive on earth to seas boiling with fury and danger. Perhaps they are born into the metaphorical night and cannot see beyond the fog and spume. They don't understand what is going on and there seems to be no one to help them, only the distant cries of other travelers as they sink or swim or drift away.

That being true, we must also say that whether born onto calm seas in good times or desperate seas in trying times, we are all on the ocean, and the ocean contains all of these circumstances and, sooner or later, we will all have the opportunity of meeting all possible conditions. We all hit rocks we did not know were there, encounter strange vapors we were never warned about and even eventually begin to understand that the sea, though vast, has boundaries and ends, although we don't know exactly when we come upon them.

Any port in a storm is a way of talking about the concept of refuge in perhaps a slightly new way, for here we are not talking about a form of refuge that is specifically designed as a vacation paradise or even a special, protected place that takes us *out of the ocean* into some place different. *Any port in a storm* is not about desperate failure either.

Understanding God or the divine—which is intimately tied up with the concept of *refuge*—means that we understand there is no place like that. Understanding enlightenment or awakening means that we have come to understand that unlike a desperate search for any crumb of safety, the concept of "any port" means that all ports are good in the turbulent seas of life, and that our job as sailors is to learn why ports are good and in fact, how to take this port, which shows up everywhere and is yet in no place particular, with us on every journey we make. We might call this port *seeing the true good in every moment.*

Only the true good will protect us from life by bringing us further and deeper into life. And only a port, or *practice or perspective*—for that is what we are talking about—that does that very thing, is a good enough vehicle for us to travel on. All other vehicles that promise some sort of safety that is not connected to life, that are vacations from life, will ultimately fail.

The idea of *any port in a storm* is the nondual perspective: the port we are looking for is everywhere. The port we pick, its flavor, how we manage to find that port over and over again in the darkness and despair we are all prone to, is the journey of our individual life, the style and dialect of our particular, localized life, and in that way, is the manifestation of the nondual in the particular. Thus, *our own way* is the ship of the dual on the waters of the absolute. To journey, to travel, to embark and then set sail and arrive, we need both the ship *and* the sea, the particular and the universal.

The remedy, it seems to me, is to help people from all religions remember the concept of "any port in a storm." Since humans want safety above all things, we have begun thinking there are *Jewish ports* and *Muslim ports* and *Christian ports* and so on. But there are not. There are only *God's ports, ports of awakening.* When we begin to understand this, we see that these ports are everywhere because the real is everywhere, and that understanding this truth, we find the way to safe harbors where we can celebrate our landing in our own language, in our way. We celebrate the *Passover* or the *Eucharist* or the *hajj*, all of which are celebrations of having found our way across the roiling waters of life into safe territory. Then we can look at the lights at various different ports and say with satisfaction and gladness: Look! the Muslims are celebrating their return to the holy place. Praise Allah! And look: the Jews are celebrating their liberation from the narrow place. *Holy holy holy is the Lord of Hosts!* And see: the Christians have landed because they found Christ again. Christ is risen!

In *A Society of Souls*, our school of healing and awakening, we have a number of core practices, all designed to help with the navigation of the spirit. None of these practices are about escaping from life. They are all about bringing us deeper and deeper into life, so that, learning to be deep enough in life, not separate from life, we see that everything we do and think and feel is God, is oneness itself, *is* the holy of holies. It is impossible to understand this without practice and learning how to practice in a way that does not create more separation from our own life by creating the illusion that there is someplace we can get to that is beyond life. We need to become more and more comfortable with *things as they are*.

Only when we are seated fully in things as they are can we help create change that does not ultimately hide within it the desire to escape from our lives by using the practice itself as an escape hatch. Instead, our practices expand inwardly and outwardly at the same time. They help us understand the world and ourselves simultaneously since there is ultimately no difference.

We will come to find that *inward*, which is to say our personal interior space, and *outward*, which is to say our world, are not the great demarcations we thought they were. We will find that they pale in comparison to the understanding of what life is when we are fully engaged with things as they are.

We are at a turning point in our world. We live in turbulent times, perhaps more desperate than we can even imagine. The idea is not to panic: we cannot know the outcome of every event or what events will eventually bring, for good or evil. What we can do however, is become more and more awake to life, which is to say, in theistic language, more and more awake to God's plan, to the natural inclination the universe itself has to awaken so that we can be the most beneficial and aware creators that we can be.

Let us see the ocean in its vast beauty. Let us hear the sound of distant or near storms without fear. And when we fear, let us accept even that as part of being a sailor on the wide sea of life. We may listen to our hearts and learn and arrive at the other shore, the far shore, the impossible to arrive at shore, which we will get to anyway, despite anyone's opinion. And let us realize that that shore is always underfoot, even in the deepest sea, where success and failure are one thing.

BEYOND ESSENCE:
A NEW PATH TO AWAKENING

Human beings are unique creatures. We suffer and we simultaneously know we are suffering, and we constantly create new ways we think we can avoid that suffering. One of those ways we hope to avoid suffering is the spiritual path. This is a great achievement, but it also presents some great problems.

Speaking for myself, though I think this is true of most people who choose to walk the path of self-knowledge, I felt compelled to examine myself. I sensed that by finding out about myself, understanding the origins of my suffering, I could suffer less.

This proved to be the case. Psychological understanding brought me more and more freedom and reduced the amount of suffering I held. I also had the feeling, especially early on in my spiritual journey, that enlightenment, being with God, awakening, and so forth, would help me suffer even less. They would be the sort of "ultimate gifts" I could give myself, the antidote for all my suffering.

In fact, I believed for a long period of time that these things would elevate my imperfect humanity to a higher level, one in which suffering would be a memory. I would finally be free.

What would I be free of? The messy parts of being a person. The difficult emotions. The hard relationships. Being influenced by the past. Not knowing what to do. Feeling helpless. I even thought I might be free of physical pain, like the Buddhist monks who set themselves on fire and seemed to feel no pain. I would be in the now, and the now as I understood it then, would be clean and clear, free of what we call the "relative world," with its never-ending confusion and ability to make me suffer. In other words, I would enter a transcendent sphere, beyond the reach of everyday life.

The Buddhists call this confused, everyday world *samsara*. The Chinese, the *saha* world, or the world of red dust. We could also call it "the relative world" or the "world of duality," and it was this world that enlightenment was going to fix once and for all, leaving the dim light of the relative behind for the glow of the absolute, the perfectly unified existence of the so-called now.

Beneath this approach, of trying to find transcendental oneness and reject the relative, are some basic misconceptions about the spiritual path which ultimately lead to deep spiritual problems. The major problem is that in our effort to gain this magical state of enlightenment, we split the world into two parts: the part we think is spiritual and the part we think is simply pain. The part we want to avoid and the part we want to go after. So based on this thinking, we go after what we think enlightenment is made of. True enlightenment, on the other hand, refuses to split the world into "pure" and "impure," or the "absolute" and the "relative." When we don't know this deep down in our bones, we tell ourselves we are after "the essence" of existence: the world's essence and our own essence. We begin to think we are on a journey to find the "secret ingredient," the altered or mystical state, something pure, pristine and perfect. Enlightenment. But what is really hiding behind this pursuit of purity is our effort to reject many of the features of duality that we find too painful or confusing. This concept of "essence" hopes to find a sort of oneness that doesn't include all of the details of this relative world of separateness we call "duality."

One of the main, messy features of this world of the relative plane that spiritual seekers especially like to avoid is "the ego," or the personal sense of a separate self. In fact, for many spiritual people, the idea of "getting rid of the ego" remains unchallenged. We think to our self: "of course I have to get rid of the ego. It is a troublesome thing and it bars my way to enlightenment." We are looking—we think—for something that "lasts forever," that will let *us* "last forever," safe and sound in an enlightened state.

This is the heart of the problem: trying to get rid of something we look upon as "temporary," in favor of something we think of as "eternal." You can see the battle lines being drawn.

If we use the image of a river, we can see how that might set us on the wrong path: real rivers bring up images of both the eternal *and* the temporary: they are always there, and they always change. Real rivers are cyclical, going through seasonal changes. They are peripheral, in the sense that what makes a river a living thing is not only the water traveling through the central canal, but the side-show as well: the slower water at the banks allows fish to spawn, birds to forage, insects and amphibians to create life and culture. Without these, the river would simply be a deluge.

So, life is bigger than anything we can call "an essence." The very concept of an essence forever tears apart the possible union between the relative and the absolute: essence, so-called, will always be "deeper within," or "higher than that," or better or more potent in some way. This view is consistently hierarchical, forgoing one plane for the next, one experience for the next experience. Although this is true—we do move from one rung to the next in life as on the spiritual path—it is not the whole truth. The whole truth can *only* be found by looking at the whole of anything.

Wholeness is always what is in front of our eyes. We refuse to see this because there is something in us telling us that what we are looking for is "deeper," or "far away." How does all of this relate to awakening, and especially a "new path to awakening"?

For many years I have been saying that the human ego, or sense of a separate personality, should not be ignored, transcended, done away with, seen through, or otherwise wasted. I have suggested that the ego is only a problem when it is not healed or integrated into the being, and that wholeness cannot be found by cutting away parts of ourselves. I have further said that the healed ego is beauty itself and that rather than making a mistake over and over again, the universe keeps making egos because that's what the universe is: the urge to be, united with the *before-the-before*, the great silence.

I used this metaphor: when part of our body does not hurt—let's say our left earlobe—we do not even know it is there. Only when a part is injured in some way do we notice its existence as a separate entity. Otherwise, it is included in the whole, invisible, useful, going about its business in silence. When our intestines don't hurt but work correctly, we don't notice them. The same with the heart, the kidneys, and yes, the mind and consciousness as well. There is something about the whole of us that is invisible and silent when we are not in pieces.

This goes for the ego as well. When the ego is healing in a deep way, it no longer whispers and yells, comments and unnecessarily protects. Instead, it appreciates, doing whatever commenting and protecting it needs to do when there is something real to do it to or with. This ego becomes a servant or a personal assistant, eager to point us in the right direction. It does not become a dictator or take over or declare itself king or queen, forever separate from its kingdom.

My point then, is to point out how any path to awakening *must* include the ego-personality, taking its health and well-being into account, realizing that without the ego being brought back into the fold of the bodymindspirit, we cannot have true awakening and true enlightenment. Without this part of the whole, true union becomes impossible. Potential and vital allies—like the ego—are left as enemies.

Awakening and enlightenment—being with God, to use other words—*without* this part of our humanity, is a sham and a shame. Something is simply lost when we erase the relative in its entirety. Daily life is the working out of enlightenment, the *action* of awakening, and without that, we simply have beings who have had one good experience or the other and are riding that experience as if it were the world. It is not.

Let me make an additional important point: it is possible to re-think the entire approach to the spiritual path by understanding that at the base of our consciousness there is a sense of an un-analyzable individuality. This individuality is not the neurotic sense of being a separate person, separate from everything, but the subtle yet powerful sense of *point of view itself.* It is silent. It does not seek to enhance itself or to get ahead, but is silently, constantly there, with no demanding content, but a simple, golden presence. It is the machinery of fulfillment.

All the activities of our consciousness are an expression of this individuality: each person's knowledge, feeling, and volition possess qualities unique to the person. We could say that this quiet center is actually responsible for the phenomena of consciousness itself and then goes on to manifest as each person's appearance, speech, and behavior. In other words, Reality, God, whatever we want to call it, in its infinite ability to express, creates this central perspective and organizes something we call "consciousness" around it.

This is truly fantastic! Not only is the ego-personality a *feature* of reality, but the central characteristic or mode of being that reality *itself* creates. Let me put this into other words and let's call this sense of ego *the natural self*, to distinguish it from the historical, un-healed, wounded, egoic self.

Reality, as we understand and relate to it, exists because there is a central point from which to view it: we call that central point "our self," or "our individuality." This natural sense of individuality is not neurotic, illusory or a mistake. This means that any true spiritual path must take into account this eternal sense of self that lies at the bottom of our consciousness. Even more important, it means that any true spiritual path must work to *heal this sense of self, this self that has been wounded by misinformation, neglect, miseducation and disregard*, so that it can reveal the natural self, which is there all along.

When we *do not* do that, but search from some idea of spiritual health that disregards the ego-self, the natural self, we are again looking for some *essence* that is separate from who we are, trying to cut away parts of ourselves to find the secret rather than doing what is necessary, which is to open our hearts to reality-as-it-is.

Opening our hearts to reality-as-it-is, is often the hardest thing for a spiritual seeker to do. Opening our hearts does not mean we do not change our behavior or challenge our feelings and thoughts. Quite the contrary! In fact, unless we open our hearts to reality-as-it-is, we *cannot change.* We are then in a battle from which we can never emerge victorious because we are fighting against ourselves.

Finally, let me be very clear: clearing away the relative plane—cultural conditionings for example—is very important at a certain point in the spiritual path. But unless the relative world is seen on an equal plane with the absolute, unless the many are seen as holy as the one, then we never arrive at the great secret: that the many and the one are a single thing; that the personal self in its heal(ing) state and the transcendent state are a unity and not in opposition to each other.

How does this affect all of us? Well, it means that we can use what we have; that we are not lacking anything we really need to start, continue or conclude—if such a thing were possible—the spiritual path. It means that there is no garbage on the spiritual path; that everything is useful. This means our suffering is useful. It means our boredom and tiredness are useful. It means our resistance is useful. Our failure, our sorrow, our courage are useful. Singing is useful and silence is useful.

It turns out that the so-called "essence" is really everywhere. There is no place that is not essential. It means that we are *already holy*, and that to experience our own holiness and the holiness of the world, we need to get out of our own way so that eventually our hearts and our self are identical.

What the heart wants to do—which is to touch the world—is identical with what our natural self wants to do, which is to touch the world, too. This means that even if we feel lost, that that lost-ness is the *real* illusion. Finding ourselves is always only one step away, not even a step. It simply means looking directly at our self and seeing what is there at the moment. The rest takes care of itself.

This is the principal journey and the central healing of the spiritual journey, the healing of the self so we are clear enough to see the way things actually are.

This is why we must go on this journey, a journey that completely changes us from a sleeping neurotic to a healing one, one who awakens to who they are, exactly as they are, neurotic or not; one who is utterly changed by being themselves for the first time, empty of prior, limiting concepts. This is the bounty and harvest of reality that is ours to enjoy. It embraces everything, including our limitations and neuroses. Its oneness includes duality because it is awakening.

The ego does not disappear. What disappears is the reasons for it to be neurotic, which is to say *out of context, separate from the whole*, working against the program of waking up. The healing ego returns home, there no longer being a reason to stay away. The addition of egoic healing to the spiritual path is very, very important. Because of it, we see that the relative plane must be healed and not ignored.

We are at an evolutionary moment here in the West. We have the possible union of personal psychological thought with the wisdom of the East's approach. A real nondualism needs both.

There is a Zen koan that goes like this:

A monk asked Zhao Zhou "Why did the ancestor come from the West?" This is another way of asking *What is this all about? Why meditate? What is Zen?* Zhao Zhou answered: "The cypress tree in the garden."

Can you feel that? Can you feel reality swirl around that tree and within that tree? Are *you* that tree? Am I? That tree contains the universe. In Kabbalah, that tree is called the Etz Chayyim, the Tree of Life.

We must all help each other along the true path, the decent path. Oneness at every turn. Choice at every turn. No relative only, no absolute only. We don't need those traps. They are not opposed but benefit from each other, the way sound and silence dance, making music.

BEING WITH GOD
EVERY MINUTE

In "The Book of Serenity", a Chan Zen collection of Zen mondo or dialogues, we find this line from a longer poem:

Pines are straight, brambles are crooked,
Cranes are tall, ducks are short.

When asked about what he had learned from his studies in China, the great Japanese teacher Dogon said "I returned empty-handed, but open-hearted. I also learned that the nose is vertical and the eyes horizontal." Open-heartedness is the endpoint of every religious or spiritual quest. Without this, what is the use of study?

We need to ask ourselves what open-heartedness really is. Is it a feeling that makes us feel good? That helps us tell our self that we are on the right path? Or is open-heartedness an action? Is it an altruistic attitude, thinking of others above the personal self or can it equally be seen as selfish, putting our own self and others on the same plane?

Sometimes when I sit in meditation, I end up saying "This is nice, and that is nice too." The whole world then seems to be a tangible, concrete, living example of enlightenment, or God-realization. Nothing but itself and the way it works. Being with God every minute means you can't force God to stay in your own house. But if your house is the world, then everywhere you sit, God is seated too. Cranes are tall, ducks are short. To that I would add: this is nice too.

In every direction we look, there are insurmountable obstacles to being with God. We are imperfect. We were programmed imperfectly and often disastrously by our parents, our culture, and our own make-up. Consequently, we have great trouble seeing reality as it is.

If we believe that we need to work through all of our neuroses in order to see reality or be with God, we are pretty much lost: *our neuroses are endless.* We can't go back and live all of our early life over again, in some perfect way, and then, being totally healthy, see God or reality. The truth seems to be much more simple: being with God is our natural birthright and not a mystical or super-human achievement. The only necessity for being with God every minute is a change in attitude, and attitude is the only thing we *do* have control over.

To understand this, let's consider the example of an incurably blind person who was trying to pretend he wasn't blind. In such a case, he wouldn't set up his house to accommodate his condition. Then, in his denial, he would constantly bang into things, knock things over, and so on. If such a person went into therapy, the therapist would not focus on fixing his eyes, but on helping him to come to grips with the reality of being blind. Successful therapy would mean that he would set up his environment so that his life could flow smoothly, so that he could be in the flow of life as who he truly was: a blind person.

Seen in this way, undergoing therapy or some other form of self-analysis would really be a process whereby we could become open-hearted to our condition, *no matter what it was*: our imperfections and limitations, our pain and our suffering.

It's true that through this process of self-understanding many of our confusions would clear up, but something even more important would be going on: through sharing our pain and being given assistance, we would come to a place, after much hard work, where we could *accept ourselves* and not be thrown or shattered by being who we actually are—in totality—*with our faults*. We would come out of the egoic program of trying to recapture a fantastical Eden and enter the concrete approach of learning to be real.

It is at this point that the possibility of being with God every moment becomes a reality and not a pipe dream. When we know *and no longer fight the fact that we are imperfect*, we can concentrate on our *attitude* toward the facts of our life. In a sense, when we know this, we have nothing to hide and nothing to defend.

This state is called open-heartedness because it brings us into the now. Only in the now can we be tenderhearted enough to be with God. This is the gateway. From this perspective, God is so small, so intimate, that we miss seeing God if our heart is closed. God can only fit in the hollow of our heart.

However, having an "open heart" does not mean to be "happy." It does not mean to be "spiritual," or wise, or anything at all. It means to have an *open attitude* toward ourselves, which is essentially a knowing and kindly feeling toward ourselves.

It means that we are no longer captivated by trying to be better, but—as a matter of course—are able to always depend upon ourselves to clean up our own messes. We bandage our wounds and the wounds of others, pray for assistance for ourselves, and give help to others because they are in the same fix we are in.

In other words, the *follow-up* is more important than the "perfected state"—if there is such a thing—in which we imagine that we would not get into trouble in life because we would see reality so clearly as to avoid every pitfall with our enlightened behavior. This sort of enlightenment is the ego's spiritual dream and does not include the real bones and stones of which true enlightenment is made.

The hard work of truly awakening seems to involve getting a clear idea of just how much we *cannot* hold all of reality—of how much of life we cannot bear. We need to see how limited we really are. Having done that, we have the chance to meet God in reality and not in the fateful fantasy of saving or punishing ourselves.

The process of learning about and embracing our limitations is not about false humility or being somehow "less than." Quite the contrary, this ability is the gateway to our true greatness. It is a sort of undressing in the service of truth, a dropping of adornment in order to see the true being who is adorned with light.

When we meet God in this way, we exist in no special state, with no special knowledge, neither high nor low. Instead, we exist in *dignity*. In the way I am using this word, *dignity* means to exist *as a whole*, that is, *simply as yourself, standing on your own two feet, with no hidden agendas, but plain.* This is the language of our true nobility, and our inner holy sense awakens to this word as we hear it. The dignified work we do then is to learn to accept our suffering, or limitation, not with a sense of fatalism, but in the spirit of truthfulness and kind-hearted acceptance. We accept it because it is true, and we have come to the point where we want truth only.

This journey can be fraught with difficulty and blindness. Often, we don't even know we are suffering: our defenses are so strong, our dissociation so profound, that we are blind without realizing it. We don't know we are limited; we don't realize that we are still fighting to be bigger or more perfect than we are.

So self-investigation is essential; it begins the process of *healing our blindness by self-knowledge*. We need to get to know ourselves. Then, we begin to know we are suffering and that we are blind.

It is vital to understand, however, that though this process of learning goes on forever, and as good and important as it is, it can *never* bring us to that feeling of being with God every moment. This is because the ego believes—even while it is getting healthier and less blind—that only *success*, *knowledge*, and *knowing* can bring us into God's presence, as if being with God was an achievement, like scaling Everest.

Being with God is a nondual state. This means it can never be achieved by choosing only one side of reality in reaction to a less preferred condition or state. We cannot see the whole of reality by splitting it further into what we like and what we do not like. *Only* knowing, *only* seeing, *only* control, can never do the job.

At some point, we need to get healthy enough to experience the humility and surrender that comes from knowing for certain that the job of clearing neurosis is endless and *will never be fully achieved*. And as we understand this, we need to fully embrace our remaining imperfections in the *certainty* that we are capable of righting our own wrongs, making amends, and repairing our mistakes. Through this new understanding, we begin to see that there is no real impediment to being with God; that we are fully capable of re-awakening from our habitual spiritual sleep over and over again. We see that even failure or blindness are no impediment to spiritual enlightenment. This is a basic change in *attitude* and focus.

Attitude is something we can rely on: we can always revisit our attitude; we can always correct it if we lose our perspective. We can regroup, think about things again, and come to new conclusions. We can firm up our resolve and cleave to God in a way that is not dependent upon grace or colored lights or secret knowledge or special dispensations.

This attitude is what ecstasy is truly made from: not something or some state separate from fear or faults or imperfections, but something that *includes* those things in the price of being human. When the nineteenth century Indian sage Ramakrishna was dying and was asked by his disciples to ask the Divine Mother to cure him, he reported back that his sickness was the way the Holy Mother was "playing through his body." When the Zen teacher Shunryu Suzuki was dying, he said at one point that sometimes death is the best teacher.

Ecstasy is *chosen by choosing the right attitude.* This is what bliss is: dignity and respect. We can keep this dignity even within our imperfections and failures by having a high regard for our own struggle. When we develop this attitude, we begin to experience other people in an entirely new way. Our life and their lives intersect and touch in the most intimate way.

We become more human—and that is the only thing that counts. We write our own epitaph by the way we live. To have the words "He lived a fully human life" inscribed on my headstone would mean that I had done well, that I had achieved my heart's desire.

Let me say finally that God is human. God may be other things as well, but we shouldn't forget that for humans, God is human. We—God and us— are in essence one thing. God is the same as us, doing the things we can do. This is not sacrilegious but liberating. God can be depended upon to do the same work we are called upon to do. Therefore, we can only know the mind and heart of this God if we are willing to be as human as God is.

To be fully human is not to throw ourselves away. *Being* human, we *often* throw ourselves away. But being *fully* human, each time we do that, we find ourselves again, we retrieve ourselves from whatever pile we have consigned ourselves to and, picking ourselves up, walk ourselves back to the tenderhearted awareness that God is with us every moment. Being awake to all of this, we *are* God, we are *with* God, and we are doing our best.

Then we are no longer simply or only *"personal people,"* being tossed this way and that without restraint or care. The graduation to "truly human" is the culmination of our birthright, the crown of creation. As *human* people, we are part of a way the universe looks at itself. When we see from this vantage point, we see only other hearts, people on the identical journey to becoming their true selves.

When we have no territory to defend, God rushes in to where God always was. It is a paradox we understand as we embrace life fully.

WHAT IS REALLY THERE

"Objective reality" is—evolutionarily speaking—a late-stage design element or perspective, created by the particular type of consciousness sentient beings have. We could say this consciousness, with its specific physical structures, has *invented objective reality in its own image* rather than *discovered* something that was always there. "Discovered" implies that there *is* something called objective reality (that it is objectively real rather than just a perceptual rearrangement) and we have finally stumbled upon it. All of that sort of thinking only arises within the model of objective reality.

Instead, the creation of objective reality should be thought of as a kind of achievement rather than some sort of truth. To put it even more correctly, before consciousness as a *platform-perspective* arrived on the scene, the universe did not have "objective reality" but only the endless accommodation of the plenum to infinite perspectives. Without sentient beings, the universe would not have exhibited this perspective and all that comes from it. To look backward as it were and use the language of this rather new idea to explain something that did not contain this idea is a teleological mistake. Objective reality only exists within the perspective and peculiar conditions of mind. The mind and its consciousness then, is the universe's partner in creation. And to make matters even more subtle, the complexifying dynamics of the universe *tend toward the creation of sentient beings*, so the achievement of objective consciousness is in some sense inevitable.

There is every reason to believe that consciousness is not finished with its evolution and that objective reality will eventually give way to some next paradigm. An example of that new paradigm is the change in consciousness that many spiritual aspirants have experienced: it continues objective consciousness and nests that in a larger, more unifying paradigm. From this perspective, trying to explain what awakening or enlightening consciousness is like from the objective/subjective model is like trying to explain diamond to coal: they are clearly connected and even made of the same material, but one is of an entirely different order *while simultaneously* being exactly the same thing. We can also get a glimpse of this next paradigm by thinking in terms of a relational universe. Here is an example.

While reading a police procedural novel by Richard Price the other night, I came across a two-word description

of a character's good quality as "Apache forbearance." This
led me to look up what this Apache quality was. I came
across this list—one from the perspective of "Anglos" and
one from the perspective of the Apache, of what qualities a
great leader should have:
Anglos:
- Has experience in office
- Energetic and aggressive leader
- Faithful to spouse
- Forceful public speaker
- Moral character
- Talks about nation's problems
- Honest
- Younger than 60/65 years of age
- Remains calm and cautious
- Has solutions to problems
- Served in the military

A similar list from the Apache might look something
like this:
- Industriousness
- Generosity
- Impartiality
- Fairness
- Forbearance
- Conscientiousness

Setting aside stereotyping and idealization, the interesting thing about these two lists is how the first emphasizes *independent, personal skills,* skills which are found *within the person themselves,* and then *used* by this person to lead. The Apache version highlights *relational qualities,* which is to say, the quality of interaction between two or more people or groups. They are qualities that appear only in interaction.

Awakening and enlightenment cannot be said to be any "thing" at all. The objective model, which has worked so well for sentient beings, allowing us to explore and create, seems powerless in the world of relational, co-arising interaction, especially in which these conditions or power do not exist until they are used.

Enlightenment is a thing *in action,* as the Tibetan teacher Chogyam Trungpa said. It is not a state but a decision-in-every-moment to both see and be part of the greater flow—a form of oneness that, at the same time, maintains separateness and individual freedom. From this perspective, it might be possible to talk about awakening or enlightening consciousness in a way that is not abstract but earthy. I say "earthy" as a metaphor for a totally integrated system, a *gaia-ic* interpenetration of uncountable events and things.

When I was younger, I often thought that enlightenment brought with it a sort of knowledge of everything; that it took *chance* out of the equation and— thinking of it as a being itself—was not frightened by life because it *knew*. It knew life's directions and goals and parted the mystery of the unknown the way a flashlight parts the darkness.

Now I understand that the perspective that awakening brings is of an entirely different order. In a sense, awakening's wisdom is the wisdom of forgetting. In our human consciousness, conditioned by the subject/object split, intent on highlighting the personal self in exclusion to the environment, everything we see is compared for a moment with a prior image we have in our mind's eye, a mixture of suppositions unconsciously posited by our culture, education and the very structure of our psyche.

This process of comparative intelligence has served our human race abundantly. Yet, at its core, it is a state of anxiety: the anxiety of survival and the need to know what we are up against at any particular moment since there is the omnipresent existential threat of *not-being*.

So, the first thing we can say about true wisdom, or awakening consciousness, is that there is a relaxation of the reflexive instinct to use comparative intelligence as the *only* measure of what will protect us from harm. Of course, in even the best of possible circumstances, this must be understood for what it is: a successful defense against an immeasurable, inscrutable and arbitrary universe that does not seem to take our personal survival into account.

But true awakening goes further. Rather than supersede comparative intelligence as obsolete in face of the newer and more unitive *intelligence of the heart*, awakening takes both the consciousness that metaphorically arises from the heart and the intelligence whose home is metaphorically directed by the head, as valid human activities and positions. It does not send our younger brothers and sisters home in disgrace, ignoring their proven value, but honors their part in the human armamentarium, ready to use even this singular intelligence when the moment is right.

So, because of the emotional and mental relaxation that comes from having another perspective to balance the stringencies of a survival consciousness that purely separates subject and object because of the benefits that sort of thing brings, a form of spaciousness is created that could be called a kind of forgetting, but which we could also call *not paying attention*.

When we forget conceptualizations and comparisons as our first line of defense against our fears for survival, we exist, in a sense, at the ready to interact, but in a conceptual space in which we are not constantly defining, waiting, self-reflecting and anticipating what will come next. Again, because this paradigm is one in which opposites are both included in the same *moment-space*, we accept all the other human abilities, including self-reflecting, anticipation, fears for survival and so on. Now however, this first consciousness has a background or, put another way, this first consciousness can now continue to exist but recede to equality with the consciousness that brings unity, so that choice becomes *choose-able* rather than something that is thrust upon us by our fears of non-existence.

In trying to understand the nature of awakening, one must consider the nature of these opposites. In the first, more common type of consciousness, choice is made by first discovering the opposites and then choosing which side we are on. An example: death in the United States has become an event almost completely out of context from its opposite, life. Death is seen as the enemy of life and not its solution and resolution. Built around this philosophy, life at any cost has become the norm for many people.

This is understandable. My own birth family religiously followed this principal to the extent that the death of my father at ninety-one years old, demented, uncomfortable, often in pain and confusion after a long and successful life, was seen as a catastrophe and not as a sad celebration of what was and what will be for all of us. It was a fear-generating occurrence. Consequently, the event of his death was a lesson for only some in my family. It was approached as a continuing metaphor and example of the caution we must live by to keep death at bay. (My apologies if I have, through lack of discussion about these issues, inadvertently defamed any member of my family who has given this serious consideration.)

I have great sympathy for this perspective. When I think about my wife dying, death seems to me like the enemy and anything I can do to be cautious and, in that way, extend her life, seems to me like a good idea. Yet, if I do not see life and death as opposites, but as equal partners, then I must place myself and all beings in the same boat and begin to come to terms with this flow and find within this flow *even more of the life I so highly prize.* To see existence itself as existing because non-existing also exists, is not only true, but freeing. Though I will be sad and even devastated if my wife dies, I might also be able to raise my arms in thankfulness that this great expanse of darkness we call God created the being who filled my life with so much joy.

At all times, wisdom-consciousness, awakening, enlightening, is relational, a relational-ness that is unbound and unafraid to connect with all that is. This means, to underscore the insight that even the smallest parts of our psyche, the fearful and sad, the limited and isolated, are related to as well.

When I see someone in my healing room, I always try to remember this truth: *that person is me. Those problems are mine.* Unless I do that, I cannot help to the degree that I would like to help. If somehow, swimming in the self-congratulatory sea of unitive consciousness, I separate myself from those who come to see me in any way, I lose the intimacy and presence that are other terms for the awakening I am aiming at. Yet, this is not about being humble or modestly assuming I don't know anything or have not achieved some degree of awakening consciousness after over forty years of travail. Unless I hold both truths, I am leaving something out. And if I leave something out, awakening consciousness disappears. Or let's put this in the best possible way: unless I hold both, I begin to remember *only* my *own* awakening consciousness. This type of "remembering" splits my consciousness as the ego's penchant for self-reflection unconsciously takes over from a fuller view. By holding both however, I actually forget to look at myself and in my "ignorance" I swim in the space in which I *and* the other exist. That is the space in which the healing of the human soul takes place.

Because we are all in the thrall of comparative consciousness, when we ask the question *What is there? What is real?* the only answer that satisfies us is that there is some "thing" there. But in awakening consciousness, we see that there is *no* "thing" there, nothing "objective" we can hold onto or creep into. Instead, there is something ineffable but potent, invisible but enthralling, reasonable in the highest degree. It is something we can live but cannot touch and, like friendship, affects our lives though we cannot find it, quantize it or tell its color or size.

So, what is really there always remains to be seen and can only be known by partaking, by living it through. And when we do partake, it leads to more wind through the trees, more water in the brook, more friends on hand, more trouble, sometimes more pain, but overall, more happiness to be what we already are: part of life, forgetful of who we are and in that forgetting, finding our true nature and intent.

WHAT CONSCIOUSNESS
DOES

We are here. We seem to be here. We are not sure where *here* is, exactly. We don't always like being here: it is sometimes difficult, sometimes painful to be here. Yet, for all its difficulties, we don't want to *leave here*. We want to be here as long and as much as possible.

The entire drama of spiritual inquiry takes place *within* the sphere of consciousness. Rather than concentrate on the specialized area of consciousness called "the ego" or the "personal self," here I'd like to focus on the entire sphere of consciousness itself, of which the personal ego is just a specialized feature.

We cannot see or perceive consciousness because it is almost completely colorless. Like a bowl of water that takes on the color of even the smallest drop of ink, this invisible consciousness disappears as it takes on the coloration of whatever it is focused on. It is more like the quality of humidity: it enters into all things while it itself remains invisible. And just as humidity enters cloth and paper, wood and iron, causing different reactions in each of these things, consciousness enters every sphere as well. In all the human worlds—the emotional, psychological and even physical self—the true shape of consciousness, the "I of consciousness" itself remains hidden behind—or more correctly *within*—the content of that particular sphere. In other words, the "I of consciousness" hides within the emotional, the psychological story or even the body. We might say that the I-of-consciousness *bends* gracefully to submerge itself within the material, perspective or action of whatever is.

Because we usually are identified with the unhealed egoic part of our consciousness, that narrow and specialized part of the psyche that says "me," and that divides the world into background and foreground, we are usually only involved in the *content* of consciousness—the coloration, if you will—and not consciousness itself. We could say the ego-consciousness is not interested so much in the I-of-consciousness as it is in the *content* of consciousness, its particular coloration. Most of the time the unhealed ego is not as interested in the vastness of impersonal space as it is in the content of the world that will affect and impinge upon it. Consciousness as an open presence itself is nowhere to be found—unless the unhealed ego thinks it is interesting for reasons of its own!

From this perspective, growth on the spiritual path consists of constantly getting the bigger and bigger view, moving from the view of the content of consciousness, to the view of the personal *egoic-I,* to a view that can see the personal self clearly because it sees the larger context that holds and co-arises with the personal self. It is then we begin to see that the personal being is held within the context of a larger form of consciousness simultaneously as this larger context leaves its mark of the impersonal vastness within our personal self. We no longer wonder which came first, the personal self or the transcendent, impersonal self. We see that they are inextricably linked: Self and non-self arise at the same time. This is the path of awakening, *the exquisite path.*

To have this happen, and eventually to see the full shape of consciousness itself, we must constantly extricate ourselves from reactivity to the content of life. As long as we are reactive in a blind or unconscious way, which is to say an *automatic* way, we are being *used* by the small view, instead of *using* the personal, or egoic self. Let's put this another way: we are letting the tool decide the job instead of the job deciding which tool to use. When this happens, we lose ourselves in the drama of the small—which after all is the seat of drama in our consciousness. Then we cannot see the forest for the trees or the trees because of the branches or the branches because of the twigs. In other words, we lose perspective. This is the trap of reactivity: to limit our possibilities.

To lessen our reactivity, that instinctual and habitual reactive relationship with life that we all have, we need to pay attention to all life has to offer, the good and the bad. We need to work through personal fears, angers, misconceptions and false beliefs. It means we need to devote ourselves to the unending process of exploration. I say "devote ourselves" and not "perfect ourselves" because the concept of perfection is limited. It posits an end point and, because it does that, it changes the journey entirely, holding some mythological future time as the most important time and skewing our vision of what it means to be alive and to practice. Like a musician who is willing to practice not only to become a better player, but because practicing *itself* is music, so too does the spiritual explorer need to walk the path because *that is what he or she does.*

The devotion itself to "filling up the well with snow" as the old Zen saying goes—an impossible task—paves the way to more transparency and flexibility, to more non-reactive openness to the sum total of life. As we do this, the hard edges of the egoic self melt a bit and soften our limited and hard view. We can use another metaphor for what happens: we begin to see the larger context of life and—like a jig-saw puzzle piece we found on the floor with no picture of what the puzzle will look like when it is done—we begin to relate that piece to other pieces on our table and slowly we see the context. The full picture self-assembles because things seem to fit together if we trust them to fit together. We can put this even another, more accurate and more profound way: as we devote the personal self to the practice of life, we forget the personal self in a healthy way. This happens naturally, like stepping back from a close-up view of a leaf and seeing the many leaves on the branch and the many branches and the many trees and the forest and the land around the forest...and so on. We begin to make room for the transcendent perspective, the view in which we find that behind all appearances lies a vibratory hum that fills the universe and *is* everyone, even as it *belongs* to no one, that resides equally in tree and sky, hatchling and child. All the colorations the I-of-consciousness has taken on begin to lighten and disappear. What is really happening is that we are *integrating* the reactive parts of our personal self. When parts of ourselves integrate, wholeness appears as it always was, a single thing filled with the myriad forms of the universe, even including—wonderfully enough—our broken pieces just as they are.

Since our ability to feel devotion comes and goes and since our ability to feel inspired comes and goes as well, as do insight and the gifts of grace, there is only one quality we can devote ourselves to which can see us all the way home: honesty. Honesty is the one transcendent quality human beings can actually achieve. Being honest does not mean that one no longer has neuroses or problems. It simply means that we are not (as) blinded, entranced or captured by them. Conflict within our self may exist, but we are not automatically fooled by it. This takes much work, but the end result is the experience of being a human being *with* a history *without* being caught unduly by that history, a human being who even sometimes gets caught but soon learns to extricate themselves into the freedom of a wholeness that includes everything.

This colorless abode is one of the reasons our personal consciousness can exist. We might call this colorless place *nothingness*. From my understanding, personal self-awareness itself exists because our sensory input—the information flowing into us from our neural network—is constantly comparing or checking this information against the background of this non-existence, this *nothingness*. In other words, consciousness is not a "thing" but a result. It is the result of *being* and *non-being* held simultaneously the way we see the scene of the field that lies beyond the staves of picket fence as we move past it at high speed, in a car for example. For many of us, this *nothingness* of the transcendent arises in our consciousness as the concept of death. This is what makes the consciousness of death so important to have. When we know how to use it, life and death are the measure of all things and from the comparison that happens through our sensory input, we come alive in a unique way, not as stones or animals are alive, but as fully—or potentially fully—self-aware beings who *know* they are seeing, who *know* they are knowing. Who *know* they are living and will die. The more we know this, the more alive we are.

This flickering moment between the great darknesses of *before birth* and *after life* is more precious than can be explained. It is precious because *something different* happens here than happens in any other realm of the universe. It is the coming to the surface of the ocean and gasping for air, filling the lungs with oxygen and singing. It is suddenly for the first time seeing that there is an ocean. We know this because we have broken through the surface into a new medium, the air. The air. The ocean. The two, held together like life and death, make a third thing, which we can call self-awareness, or *tathagata,* or even God. It is only here, separate and not separate, both anguished because we are alone and hypnotized by the beauty of possible return and healing that we find in the here and now, can we see the journey to no place, that is our life. You must pay attention to this: The entire universe is in your heart and mind.

THE MYTHOLOGY OF ENLIGHTENMENT

Kasyapa, those who focus upon emptiness and have thoughts of emptiness fall far from my words. Kasyapa, to have views on the self the size of Mount Meru is tolerable, but with strong pride to have views on emptiness is not. Why is that? Kasyapa, if emptiness is that which uproots every view, then Kasyapa, I say that those who have a view on emptiness alone are beyond all cure.

— *Heap of Jewels Sutra*

In 1968, I was a college student. I had begun meditating by reading a book about Zen and started practicing every day, sitting in my bedroom facing a bright blue wall. Shutters I had made from discarded Masonite filtered the light coming in from the street below.

That day, for some reason, I felt no urge to jump off my cushion or to find out some secret or receive some new knowledge. One by one, everything that seemed important dropped away until there was *no place but here, no time but now.*

Suddenly, with a *whoosh* I actually heard, a powerful force inched up my spine and out the top of my head until it formed a kind of hood about five or six feet over my head. At that moment I didn't know if I was asleep or awake: the two states seemed to have become a single thing, a unity. I was both outside myself and deeper in than I had ever been before. The event lasted perhaps half an hour and during that time, all problems, splits, questions and anxieties simply ceased to be. It was not so much that I felt I knew the answer to anything but more like there were no longer any questions. Everything was completely whole, complete, finished, dynamic and alive. Everything was completely itself. I wrote a short poem that ended with the words *now, only to understand how to care for the prisoner hearts around me*. I began trying to live those words.

In terms of classic spiritual literature, this experience fit right in. In terms of my own growth and spiritual practice, it became part of my personal mythology of enlightenment and subtly became the experience I judged all other spiritual experiences against. Unconsciously, and even a little consciously, every time I sat down on the cushion, this was what I was after. Sometimes, using little tricks and sentences, bringing back memorable phrases or body sensations, I was able to duplicate the sensations and feeling of being *only here only now*, but little by little, the experience drifted away from me and entered another realm, something that once was, was no longer and would have to come again.

It took me almost twenty-years both to understand—and finally discard—this experience, before it ceased to be an obstacle to further spiritual understanding. *Experience* is a finely wrought two-edged sword. On one hand, we need experiences. We are personal people with our own senses, thoughts and feelings. These are the things that are changed through spiritual practice and we call these changes "experiences." Without them—especially when they have been experienced before by others, written down and shared—we have no idea if we are on the right track. Hitting the tennis ball the right way is an experience. We need to get the feel of the ball on the racket. We need to get the feel of *right here and right now* so that we learn and so that our behavior, influenced by the experience, changes. Whether we are working in a nondual tradition or a deistic tradition, many who have gone before have shared their knowledge, which is to say their experience, and they point the way to our true nature, to our God.

These experiences can become institutionalized as well. I always found it interesting that different spiritual communities have different experiences in searching for and finding the same God, in realizing their real nature. For example, in communities involved in certain types of kundalini yoga, physical movements called kriyas seem to be an indication that something of evolutionary importance is happening. In Zen communities, seasoned meditators are stiller than beginners, who might move from uncomfortable positions more easily. In Jewish houses of worship, prayer is accompanied by a swaying and rocking motion that brings the prayerful one deeper into contact with the Divine. In Christian communities, the position is often on the knees, not standing, and there is no swaying. So, experience is at once absolute within the framework of a particular practice and relative when one compares practice to practice. What does it all mean? We need experience and yet experience itself can obscure the very thing we are after: the unimpeded view.

A solution is difficult to find because there is no easy answer. We cannot banish experience because to do so would violate part of our true nature as beings-who-experience. Yet, *by not* putting experience aside, we are always seeing the past, someone else's or our own past experience, and trying to recreate it in the present. The recreation of the past is exactly what liberation or connection to God's Presence is not.

The answer lies in a deeper understanding of the *experiencer,* him or herself. If we begin to understand what experience actually is, where it comes from, where it is held, and finally *who* is holding it, we begin to acquire the freedom that is beyond having or not having experience.

I call the owner of experience the *who-is*, and the *who-is* is the subject of the next essay in this book.

THE WHO-IS

One thing is clear about the State is that It is not a world or place of abode to which the liberated ones are to go either now or after death. Very queer beliefs are being cherished and taught by different kinds of believers.

— *Maha Yoga or The Upanishadic Lore*

I began my first experiments with psychotherapy when I was eighteen years old. I was determined to find out the reason for my suffering. First, I tried traditional Freudian psychotherapy and, although I learned a powerful and interesting insight from the only time the therapist spoke, I soon continued my exploration with more modern approaches in talk therapy. Many years later, I began exploring body-centered psychotherapeutic approaches as well.

Around the same time I got involved in psychotherapy, I also began my Eastern spiritual pursuits. I studied Ramakrishna's teaching. I read about Ramana Maharshi and spent hours asking, "Who am I?" I did yoga and played the sitar and began my earnest study of Zen.

It soon became clear to me that I was dividing my life in two. On one hand, I was doing psychotherapeutic work to heal my ego. In my sessions we talked about what was bothering me and how it connected to my childhood history. There was never any mention of "enlightenment," or "awakening." My spiritual work, on the other hand, was concerned with enlightenment and awakening. Both of those words took on the role of a kind of holy grail to me and, through my meditative and spiritual work, I tried to reach them.

Through each of these disciplines I had experiences. I found a sort of peace or insight through the psychotherapeutic work but never felt enlightened. Through zazen I had many *kensho* or awakening experiences, but they seemed to by-pass my history entirely and, sooner or later, despite deep universal insight, I found myself forgetting what I had found and back once more in the mire that brought me to therapy in the first place. I could not understand why the light I had found faded so quickly or why the open-hearted feelings I sometimes got through therapeutic understanding did not give me a sense of transcendent, universal consciousness. And though I sensed that there must be a connection between the two approaches and the two seemingly different responses I had, more often than not I alternated between the two, never sure where I should come down or how the two were connected.

Likewise, with the notion of God. Having been brought up Jewish and living with a Western mindset, I was deeply connected to the concept of God as a separate being. This Being was someone I could relate to but who, at the same time, rarely seemed to relate to me. And while I sometimes felt judged by this absent God, I also felt abandoned. When I called out, I only heard a great silence from heaven. And yet, when all was said and done, I needed this spiritual friend called "God," someone to guide me, to ease my pain, to help me through the increasingly rough times, especially through my late teens and early twenties.

While Judaism talked about prayer, surrender, invocation and evocation to a seemingly separate divine figure, my nondual Buddhist and Advaitic studies talked about "the self," "knowledge," self-inquiry, meditation and the answer to the question "Who am I?" No mention of God. No mention of a separate divine being, just the end result of some form of illumination. The separateness that was the hallmark of the path of prayer—God and me— seemed to be the very problems that the nondual approach was trying to heal. How to be separate and relate to God and be one with the universe at the same time? How to merge with the beloved (which seemed warm and intimate) and find the self (which seemed austere and universal). That was the problem.

Investigating and trying to live these opposing views was not theoretical to me at all. It seemed to be a matter of life and death. The great difficulty I faced came from the fact that sometimes I needed one approach and sometimes I needed the other. Again, this was not just an intellectual predilection. Praying to God, trying to be more moral or open-hearted or, in short, more or less of something I already was, usually worked for a while and then got me tangled up in being dissatisfied with myself, feeling less than, feeling I would never arrive and finally sinking, despite pleas to God and the angels, into despair. Then—opening up to the opposing view—I would see that I needed to lay all of my concepts and philosophy aside and actually be where I was. I needed to extricate myself from the thinking mind and stop my constant quest to "get better," to be more. In this paradigm, I felt I needed to see through the source of my problem, the concept of "I," and expand into the spaciousness of is-ness. That too would last for a while until my heart began to yearn for the warmth of knowing I was held in a loving God's arms. Nondualism seemed too cool to me, arctic, and non-relational. My heart was my guide and my heart was in two pieces.

There was another, even more subtle division in my thinking that played into all of this as well: I had a deep sense in myself that everything in life, in fact everything in the universe, was divine, or holy, or whole and complete as it was. In my best moments, this resulted in a revelatory feeling of the perfection of the moment, with its imperfections and mistakes and ignorance, its nobility and beauty as well. From this view, trouble was invited in when I was separate from that understanding and relied on preference and thus split the world asunder, losing the miraculous sense of the ordinary. Effort, in this scenario, was to let go to the moment, to the now, to things-as-they-are. At the same time, I was acutely aware of my many imperfections and limitations—including my grandiosity as a reflexive movement away from sense of worthlessness. I knew I needed to improve, to work hard to get better, to not accept my life as it was but to investigate my many misdeeds and make amends. Again, this split between an effort to be and an efforting to do.

Beside psychotherapy, with which I was already engaged, I felt I—as a separate being—needed a "higher being," whether that being was God, Jesus, a Buddha or a mantra, or some deity or some more experienced spiritual friend. Letting go of concepts, just sitting, pure meditation gave me freedom from my over-busy mind. It quelled my anxious mental body. But it did not seem to affect my heart or make me a more loving or better person. I still felt emotionally stiff, somewhat distant, suspicious and protected. Prayer on the other hand, whether to what I understood as God or to Jesus or some other deity, or singing to Rama or Krishna as another example, opened my heart and seemed to heal my emotional outlook. I felt happier, but no more enlightened. Enlightenment versus open-heartedness. Joy versus vision. This was the spiritual seesaw I rode for twenty years as I tried to reconcile these two poles of the spiritual dimension and as my need for each alternated.

The reconciliation of these two paths became my path. I wanted an enlightened heart and an intimate mind. Enlightenment *and* heart. Having one or the other simply did not suffice for the sense of spiritual justice that lived intently within me. I felt the two had to be one if either one of them was to be taken as true.

Over the years as I healed, through intense psychotherapy with kind and attentive spiritual beings, and as repeated spiritual experiences brought me further and further into reality, I understood that my instinct—that everything is holy—was correct. This went for the ego as well: the ego-personality did not need to be discarded: it needed to be healed. I also discovered that my other impulse was correct as well: as eternally imperfect beings, we all need improvement. I certainly did. And this improvement of the personal self, was personal, sometimes historical work. It involved effort and digging and thinking about the past and hoping for the future, in short, all the human emotions and states pressed into service, aiming at bringing the ego-personality into the present moment.

But a question remained: Why did I alternate between these different visions of what the spiritual path should look like? And why, thinking of others, did following one or the other path exclusively cause so many seekers to miss one part or the other of the spiritual journey, either having transcendent vision and a sense of the overarching whole and yet missing the ability to be in healthy, human contact, or on the other hand, having deep psychological insight but no glimpse of the one "who doesn't come or go"?

The answer turned out to be rather simple. I began to see that my split existed because I had an "all or nothing" approach to the personal ego, the personality. In my thinking, it was either something to work on or something to ignore, something to heal or something to rise above. I could not reconcile these two views.

Slowly, I began to understand that to think of the personal self exclusively as an illusion was incorrect, and that, contra-wise, to think of it as real was ultimately misleading.

The idea of a real—and yet illusory self—is easily understood if we think of this metaphor: there is a river, broad and flowing. Near the edges of the river, nearer to the shore where the flow of the water is slower, eddies sometimes form. These little whirlpools gather into themselves the flotsam and jetsam of the river's life: bits of twig and leaf, a whirl of foam, all slowed down by a bend in the river. The addition of this material to a small whirlpool actually helps the whirlpool maintain is twirling organization better. It becomes ballast, and the energy of the river, still feeding into this small portion near the shore, helps the eddy—which, as we know, is doomed to disappear—maintain its individuality a little while longer.

The individual person is like this eddy. From one perspective, it would be wrong to say it is an illusion. It is clearly there. It traps floating material. It adds its own dynamic to the river, supporting the river's slowing its speed near the shore, where fish and turtles and frogs lay eggs, in the quieter shallows. Yet, on the other hand, it has no existence apart from the river. It is made of the river and nothing else. The water, the things that fall into the water are all part of the river and the eddy, while appearing separate for a while, is destined to return to another state where it is submerged in the whole. Then, because of the living dynamics of the whole, the inevitability and constant potential of the all, in this the river, it emerges, at some other place and time, collecting, whirling and finally, disappearing, only to arise again.

If we can call ourselves eddies for a moment, we can easily see that our separate-only consciousness, the consciousness of the eddy in full bloom, so to speak, is a valid thing but not the *only* thing. If we call ourselves only the river, then we might miss the fact that the existence of the river itself demands that eddies form, *with* their separate-only consciousness and their temporary nature.

The wonderful thing is: when we begin to see the full picture, the interplay of the absolute and the relative (to now use the real concepts we are talking about), we are not trapped by the so-called bigger or absolute view or the so-called smaller or relative view. We are free to be human beings, separate individuals, in a vast river.

The eddies form, dissolve, float and move. To say that they are separate and real is to deny what they are really made of. To say that they are only part of the river is to ignore the beauty of the small swirl and the fragments of life captured within its twirling water. Constant manifestation that comes from nothing. Multiplicity of being that comes from the one. Our personal self is like this, real and unreal, changeable from one moment to the next, and all of the various guises are still part of the whole and not to be ignored.

It was through this that I understood the *who-is* and how it naturally calls out for the right nourishment as it morphs from one perspective to the next, from one view to the other This *who-is* calls out for truly nondual food, nourishment that is keyed to its being-ness, through which it can grow into that unspeakable wholeness that is the river and its products taken as the truly One.

Sometimes we are small and separate. Our help then needs to come from the separate. When I prayed to Jesus or God, or chanted the name of Rama, or asked Ramana or Ramakrishna to help me, I was calling out from my separateness to something that seemed separate. That holy separate one always answered.

Sometimes we are wide and vast. Our help then comes from this wideness and vastness. No effort but letting go. No names but no name. No sound but silence.

Because all the *who-is's* are facets of a single thing, each time we correctly relate to who we are, without judgment but with care and sincere joy, we help that *who-is* continue on its journey of constant change. When we help the small and separate, we see its secret heart is really vast and open. When we help the vast and open, we see it also depends upon the small and particular. In this way, the who-we-are, changeable like the tides, leads us to the next step. And since each step is holy, we are never really apart from the whole. It is available in its tiny grandeur at every moment.

Each *who-is* is a path toward wholeness and a complete wholeness in and of itself. As we see the true union of the particular and the nameless all, we see that each *who-is* is transitory *and* a facet of an infinite reality. Each *who-is* is both a doorway into the infinite *and* the infinite itself.

In this way, through constant practice and constant letting go, we begin to see that the *who-is* is neither an obstacle nor the goal, but a fact of the river we are. We become less attached to any particular *who-is* as an identity, while at the same time seeing each state as a valid expression of the human self. We begin to see that when we are connected and devoted to kindness, we need to speak the language of acceptance and skillful means to ourselves before we ever utter a word of teaching to others. Our relationships with others are built upon this relationship with ourselves.

When I did not understand this, I judged myself for having many practices, or many facets within my single practice. But then I began to see this as true kindness, which seemed to be at the heart of everything. Having specialized practices which take into account varying degrees of separateness, the *who-is* gets to experience the broader or smaller view, whichever is needed in the moment. The forest is good, but the berry is likewise good. An angel for each blade of grass. These phrases began to mean something to me.

I found that this is kindness-in-action, and it was the cure for the human predicament of prejudice toward and the idealization of various spiritual states. It spoke to the misplaced idea that we should be one type of individual in all circumstances or that enlightenment was a monolithic state, a sort of stopping place instead of a "going-on place."

Eventually, as we begin to understand the journey of the *who-is,* we find there is nowhere to go, no steady "self" to turn to; no ideal image of transcendence except this: "One Law for the Lion & the Ox is Oppression," as William Blake said. We begin to see that even if our practices always look the same on the outside, true spiritual work is always new and exact, inviting the devil in one day and the angel the next, everyone a potential friend. Eventually, we believe less in the appearance of limitation and love each thing, each *who-is,* for what it is: an expression of the holy and turning world. Appearances cease to matter, except as rafts to run the river on.

We eventually find that there is nowhere to go, nothing to do but relate completely to the present moment just as it is, because each moment is the beginning of the path and the completion of the path. Each path is transformed from ignorance (when it is ignored or seen as "less than") to a thunderbolt-like, or wisdom-like, vehicle. In fact, it is beyond any wisdom-vehicle: the starting place, path and ending place are all a single thing.

When we see the various *who-is's,* we are already looking at ourselves from a new vantage point, a nameless place whose only manifestation is these various facets and changes. Our home is everywhere.

When we are a "season," we might manifest as *summer, fall, winter,* or *spring.* When we are a full person, we think and don't think, get lost and get found again, sleep and wake up again; as a manifest being, we live and die, get reborn and die again.

The changing *who-is* is intrinsic and internal to the absolute, unconditional, nameless and unspeakable part. It is not an aberration of the absolute, as if the absolute should be a monolithic, unchanging gem. Change is what makes the diamond. The great silence of the so-called absolute and the manifest world need each other to exist and have no independently existing natures. In this way, the *who-is* is neither real nor unreal. It is not a fixed thing, but the temporary manifestation that supports the absolute, which could not exist without this revolving sphere of change. This view cuts the cord between enlightenment being a single thing or "eternal," or "outside of time," or any of the million other illusions of fixedness our unhealed egos would like to have about the whole. We could say, then, that the real "absolute" is the union of this changeless place of silence and non-characteristics with the constantly changing hubbub of this revolving world. The absolute is the entire thing. What can be more inspiring than the mysterious existence of anything at all? The unvoiced and the voiced together at last as they were from the beginning.

Finally, engaging and practicing with any *who-is* in this way *automatically changes the who-is*. It allows it to evolve into less complex, perhaps less troubled, more spacious manifestations. This change is automatic: God turns his face as we do this; the wheel of the law turns, too, until there is no dharma separate from ourselves. It is this turning that seats us ever more deeply; this big-seeing and exposure to change that helps us relate to the fact we are not a "thing" at all, but a silent abode in which the world turns and whose bare hands turn the entire world as well.

THE EXQUISITE PATH:
THE HEART OF NONDUALITY

I was born Jewish and first looked to that religion to answer my questions. Then I turned to science, music, art, yoga, Tai Chi, Zen, psychoanalysis, Western spirituality and then finally back to Judaism and Buddhism through Kabbalah, Zen and the Pure Land School. God be praised! So many paths, each of them studied diligently and deeply, each with a different point of view on how to get to God, to enlightenment, to well-being, and to Wholeness.

Prayer. The questions of Who am I? and other koans in the great Chan traditions, each taking me a little further into the well of darkness, trying to find the sparkles of a starry night. I have come to believe—after all of this study—that there is a path for right now, that brings the great insights of Western psychology and the unitive approaches of the nondual paths like Advaita, Zen, and Shin Buddhism, into a mix that takes God and liberation out of the realm of fantasy and makes it not only real, but possible. Not only possible, but also inevitable. Not only inevitable but also necessary for our lives and our planet to continue. The word exquisite has its roots in the same place as the words ask, seek, gain and win. Although it is not linguistically associated with the word kindness, it is based only on that: it asks for that, seeks that, gains it, and in that way, wins the world.

The spiritual path has generally offered two distinct ways to reach oneness: one is by relating directly to oneness itself, and the other is through surrendering to a higher power. These are the paths of nonduality and duality as traditionally understood. We could also call these paths the "path of oneness" and the "path of surrender."

It usually feels as if we choose the path we are on but, in actuality, the path chooses us. Why it does this is mysterious and ultimately unknowable. The path of the warrior, the path of the servant, the path of self-reliance, the path of surrender: *they find us.*

In the path of oneness, we do various things to begin to have a glimpse of what some people call "the absolute." We try to live in the now in some manner or we begin to break down the differences between things by using some technique or meditation. We learn that all thoughts—good or bad, happy or sad—are ultimately only *thoughts*, and, seen from the right perspective, have no power over us. We discover that subject and object are not as separate as we thought.

Because nothing is left out in the path of oneness, we must also work to have a strong foundation of separateness so that any opening to the absolute is real and authentic and not an escape from the truth of our separateness. Having lived all of our lives in the relative world and having become established, so to speak, in the neighborhood, and perhaps even stuck in our ways, we need to get a glimpse of a much bigger picture. Our limiting concepts need to be broken. By learning to live in non-conceptual spaciousness, we learn to be less self-centered. We begin to search for the true self by discarding many or perhaps all of the versions of the self we have been carrying around like excess baggage for our whole lives.

This path takes tremendous courage and a good teacher since the perils of trying to teach ourselves new ways of looking are many, as our ego constantly tries to undermine the new, the real and the authentic. All of these tools, however—including the courage, the teacher, and the path itself—eventually need to be discarded as "the absolute" comes into view. Then, either by a kind of spiritual shock or just a gradual knowing, we come to see the non-identity of everything, the lack of independent self in everything, which has the benefit of relaxing our ego's constant fight against the world. We *become* the world—not in an egoic or supernatural manner, but as part of the world, not separate in any way.

Clearly, the personal is not highlighted in this path. This approach—which helps us see through the limiting concepts of difference, that is, to see things as we believe they actually are—is based on the fact that, upon examination, there is no personal to be found. All of the things we call "a self" are really "empty" of independent existence, that is, they have no intrinsic, unchangeable nature. Instead, like river and shore, they are mutually dependent upon each other for defining what they are: the river is defined by shore even as the shore makes the existence of the river possible.

It is the same with our body, feelings, thoughts, and mind itself. Every place we look, there is no individual thing or event, but rather the interlacing web of relationships, which itself has no intrinsic and permanent self. This allows us to move toward something that is impersonal in nature and beyond our small self.

It is also possible for mysterious Spirit to suggest another pathway along this journey to knowledge. This path—the path of surrender—requires a different kind of effort and a different mental attitude. Its direction is not toward oneness or the absolute, but toward the deity who sits separate from the searcher and from the searcher's quest to understand God—who is seen as being responsible for the core of the searcher's being and as the essential creator of the universe. The journey, from this perspective, is to surrender to this greater power.

This is a highly personal path that works with a personal creator God, a God one can communicate with, and who has a personal interest in the salvation of every being. It is the meeting between the person and the Personhood of God.

There is a kind of emptiness here, too, but it is the emptiness of the personal salt being dissolved in the greater sea of God: our very substance, in other words, is melted into the greater substance of God. It has ecstatic components and a kind of certainty that arises as the will of the creator becomes known, and as it becomes possible—through the surrender of the personal will—to live in the nimbus of godly intent.

The literature of the path of oneness is mostly filled with descriptions of how the personal is seen to be illusory. In the most sophisticated descriptions of the nondual state, the need for personhood or individuality is clearly described as part of the discriminating mind, that portion of reality in which the separate things of this world reside. But even here, in my opinion, the union with the personal does not go far enough; it is not "warm" enough toward the personal. To illustrate my point, let me make a provocative statement: truly understanding the oneness of creation, even in its impersonal form, should lead directly to understanding the personal creator in all of its glory. In other words, the purpose of our connection to the so-called absolute is to return to the *personal* in a new way.

Let me put it another way: being in relationship to the absolute gives you the absolute freedom to engage in relationship with everything in the universe—including the personal. The personal and the entire notion of relationship arise together. The personal cannot be avoided. To avoid it in favor of something that seems to be more transcendent—the impersonal transcendent for example—is to misuse awakening to make a hovel of what could be a mansion.

What we are trying to find is the existence of the personal within the transcendent. If we understand that clearly, we find that even when we have glimpsed "the absolute," the personal still exists in a new and mysterious form. With the existence of that personal, a *personal* force in the universe that is *personally* interested in us also arises: an exacting, impeccable intelligence that is not concerned with our small mind, slavishly restricting itself to either the self or non-self, absolute or relative, personal or impersonal, but which is free, in the way we would all like to be free. For the sake of my love for this approach—which focuses on the connections between transcendent oneness and the duality of the personal—I have called this view *the exquisite path*.

In the exquisite path, unlike in traditional nondual formulas that explain unity, what is emphasized is not the connection between things, *but their differences*. When this is done correctly, each thing in the universe becomes a *dharma* or truth; each item in creation, a Torah all its own. We look at these differences without comparison, until they become the many tongues of God, speaking God's Name as the essential identity of all the manifest things in this world.

In the Zen path, as an example of a nondual approach, when we see the emptiness of things or, put another way, when we see that all things need all other things to be themselves, we also begin to experience the *is-ness* of all things. In other words, a paradox arises: as we see that nothing exists as an independent self, we see—simultaneously—that each thing *is itself and itself only*.

Both of these realizations are important, though different and complementary. First, we see that all things are mutually co-arising; that nothing stands alone; that there is no self, in ourselves or in things, to defend. Then we see that all things are *only* themselves, each thing pristine and beautiful, each thing the most important thing in the world, the most precious. Seeing both the emptiness and the things in themselves—oneness and separateness—makes possible the birth of skillful means, as the interplay between these two facets of the world are worked through. *Having skillful means* is simply having found a way to live in this world.

From my perspective, what arises when we see this emptiness of self *and* the simultaneous *self-ness* of things is *compassion*, that perspective (not feeling) that holds the world in its delicate and timeless state, splitting nothing, but holding all. Compassion is a quality-of-being that can only be experienced once all things are seen as empty of self—and then returned to their individuality, whether pristine and clear or confused and suffering. I call this state *continuity/density* because it evokes the marriage of oneness and separation.

The first step to this is-ness on the exquisite path is to see things as they are. This is actually very easy . . . *and* very difficult. It is easy because the instructions are very simple: *see each thing as it is.* It is very difficult because human beings cannot easily do this. We always see things through our historical eyes, with our opinions and wounds, with our egoic fascinations and our personal limitations. We prefer one thing to another, one way of being over another; our preferences are usually at the service of protecting us from aspects of our past that we found too painful to bear. Our neuroses and characterological defenses have been our savior and it is very difficult for us to let go of its protection.

But the more we realize the extreme difficulty of achieving pure seeing, the more we are able to do it, the more we are able to include our lack of success in this venture as part of the venture itself. *We can then see ourselves—our limitations and failures and imperfections—clearly, and, in seeing ourselves clearly, see the world ever more clearly.* We do not defend against *what-is*, even as it includes our own problems and faults. We see what is.

Human beings, in our exclusive attachment to the historical version of our personal ego, resist this moment of seeing things as they are with all our might. It is as if there is a voice in all of us that says, "If I see things as they are, I will die. I will directly know the suffering I went through as an infant and child when I was helpless and alone, and that would be unbearable." These words are true for most of us, because our personal self—rather than being a dynamic structure in the Now—is the result of the accrual of our original nature with the wounds, misfortunes, and misinformation we have suffered. Consequently, to see things "as they are" is to see our own suffering and some of the lost self that lies beneath the debris of our hardships. So, we fear being in reality and avoid it . . . even as we long for it. But there is something stronger still than this fearful voice. Even sensing the real or imagined danger of seeing things as they are, it urges us onward none the less. This is the voice of the true nonduality, which is not neutral, unyielding, disinterested, aloof, or colorless but vital, alive and dynamic.

Clearly seen, the true nonduality we experience as we encounter both emptiness of self and *things as they are in themselves,* this condition of oneness *and* separateness, turns out to be the elixir of life itself, a magical fluid that takes on the coloration of whatever is true and speaks to that true thing in its own, personal language. It does so because we are personal creatures in every sense: that is, despite the fact that we are "empty" of a continuous, unchanging self, we are still a self, with a personal viewpoint, a limited life span, a wave upon an ocean of countless waves.

Now, "the great luminous silence" (a phrase suggested to me by the great teacher Reb Zalman Schachter-Shalomi) we once called "the absolute," forms around the seed it is given, and speaks to us in the language of *pure personal self,* the self that can be called *the personal with no history.* This is the self that is left—or returns—once we have visited emptiness and returned to the "something-ness" of this world. It is through the channel of "something" that the universe speaks to us. Buddha has a name. Jesus has a name. You and I have an original face and an original name. The true view is not causal: God does not speak and we listen. Instead, as we come into the personal-with-no-history, the God-with-no-history arises. We could also say that God—in the guise of the absolute personality, calls our personal self to realization. This call to awakening is not a case of "call and response" or reactive causality, but *simultaneous causality:* a-temporal, immediate, mutual and inevitable. We could say, for instance, that our existence awakens God as God awakens us.

This is the exquisite path, so named because it takes what is in front of it—garbage or goddess, Torah or trash—and turns it into the gold of compassionate means. Compassionate means is the body—our body and the physical presence of all things. Is-ness needs oneness to exist while compassionate means needs separation to exist. Compassion is not about oneness or merging. Compassionate means is sitting down and standing up. It is every moment of life as it is.

To enter into the so-called absolute and deny the body—that is, to come down on the side of oneness as the only and ultimate truth—is to die as a human being. This may be commendable on some other level I am not aware of, but more commendable to me is to be born for the first time, born as a human being whose personal nature is the way the universe speaks to us all. To achieve intimacy with the union of oneness and compassionate means—which is the truth of what the absolute is—the exquisite path asks you to feel the skin of someone and say to yourself, "This skin is the only skin like this in all the known universes. It will soon disappear. Its color, its irregularities, its bumps and grooves, its smoothness and texture are an exquisite combination of all the moments that have gone into making it up, exactly as I feel it right now."

The exquisite path—which is the path of duality as it is with its oneness and separation—works with the present moment as it is. It understands that the skin being touched is the product of this person's biochemistry, their childhood, their ancestors, their genes, their culture, the food they eat for those reasons, the excesses they have, their missing dreams, the dreams they have conquered and the ones they have loved, the wounds they have suffered, the ones they have dominion over, the happinesses, the sadnesses. This is the skin of this person who will never come again.

This is hard to do because all of the defenses that have protected our bodily and psychic life come into play each time we allow something outside of ourselves to simply be itself. At that moment of allowing however, the full energy of life appears, the same spontaneous, alive, involuntary, pulsation that we, our parents, their parents before them, our culture, and our species have defended against for ages.

For some of us, it can be excruciating. It takes long years of practice to allow the world to be the world without defending ourselves against it in some manner: through dissociation; through judgment; through premature or hasty action; through splitting and shattering; through overuse of intelligence or even over-attachment to silent mystery itself. It is possible to hide anywhere.

But as we see the world and ourselves—with all of our joys and fears, just as they are—as we work on our own psychology so that we can bear our own pain as it is and thereby see the world as it is, we get to see the compassionate means that is-ness works through. We get to see the body and not just the signs that the body was there. It is here that the fearless *reclaiming* of the personal comes into play. This can only be done when we have—again paradoxically—*moved beyond preference to find our preference,* because a return to choice is our destiny . . . as soon as we stop choosing! Being "one with our destiny" does not mean drifting in the wind of choiceless-ness, but finding our way to the inevitable choice. This is the fulfillment of our fate.

Let us look at the big picture: this universe seems to work in certain predictable ways. Some of these ways are physical: if we drop a stone, there is no question it will fall. Though in our magical thinking we all wish we could find someone who could make a stone stall in mid-air, this has never been the case.

Likewise, there are certain spiritual laws—we might call them laws of relationship—that seem to hold true as well. For instance, if I hold out my hand to you, you are likely to take it in yours and shake it. If I kiss you and you like it, you may kiss me back. We can raise this to an even higher level: if we love our garden, it will grow. If we demonstrate our love by weeding it and watering it, it will grow. Even further:

if we practice our spiritual discipline, we will grow in spirit. These things are true, and we have all found them to be so by experience and not because someone told us they were true.

We call a law a "spiritual law" if it holds true not only for the physical world, but for our souls as well. In this exquisite path, we begin to see the pure differences between things and simultaneously become aware that when we see the differences between things, all things start to glow with the same light. Actually, they have always been glowing: we simply did not have the eyes to see. When we are strong enough to step into *what-is* without shattering, we see this shining and it is the is-ness of all things in themselves, the oneness of the universe.

The universe is a universe of compassionate means, that speaks tenderly to us, calls to us like a mother to her child, scolds us like a mother does her child, touches us like a mother does her child: personally, with focus and intent.

Eventually, the act of seeing everything as it is—seeing that nothing is incomplete in itself, even though nothing is complete in and of itself—requires that everything, even our own preferences, be included in the great *what-is*. All must be brought into the light of knowledge.

In the beginning, this is impossible. But the path of the particular is wide and free, and as we learn of our history and it becomes possible to look directly at the altar where our humanity was sacrificed in small and big ways, we become capable of seeing things as they are.

The body changes to make this possible. The muscles and sinews, instead of armoring themselves against reality, now stretch forward, eager to see *what-is*. We become strong enough to bear our story, to see the kind of tree our winters made us, whether we are bent and scarred, beautiful and leaning, a snowy white birch, or a tattered and cracked black oak that has borne the brunt of strange and unexpected weather.

Eventually, as we practice this path, we get strong enough to enjoy ourselves as the exquisite combination we are: our boundlessness with all of our particulars. In this way, we eventually become capable of loving one another and loving each thing in its differences. We arrive at the absolute's intent, which is love and union with the particular. This love is not generalized and was never meant to be. From the vantage point of this love, the neutral aspect of the Absolute is the lowlands compared to this human, high plateau.

There is a Zen koan: Unmon said, "Look! This world is vast and wide. Why do you put on your priest's robe at the sound of the bell?"

This koan is usually thought about as being about oneness and separateness. Simply put: as all things are truly one, and since the Divine is found everywhere and in everything, why do you rely on form? Why do you rely on *this* form?

Mumon wrote a poem about this:

> *If you understand "it," all things are One;*
> *If you do not, they are different and separate.*
> *If you do not understand "it," all things are One;*
> *If you do, they are different and separate.*

But I would like to ask this question: "What is it that makes this monk put on his robe? Does his connection to form come from his love of humanity?" If it does, I would like to ask the further question: "What causes him to love?" While this koan concentrates on the training of the student, I think it says something about the nature of the universe.

To me it says that when we are freed of preference— either for oneness or duality, for the absolute or the relative—the true nature of the universe that is not within our command shines forth in the language of the personal. It speaks to us in this language so that we do not have to betray any aspect of who we are or leave any part of this universe that made us, and which is our home. The nature of the universe is kind and has within it the desire (can you admit this to yourself?) to add self-consciousness (or the personal) to self-realization, a body to mind, skillful compassionate means to the exciting fact that everything in the universe is exactly what it always was since beginningless time.

This is why the path chooses us, although we usually do not see it this way. We do not see the choiceless choice, the choice that is inevitable because the nature of the universe, and therefore our nature, is love itself. *Love—personal love—turns out to be the great impersonal force of the universe.*

When we exist only in the absolute, we cannot easily talk about the personality of the Great Mysterious Universe. Personality is what we have broken down and left behind. Personality is what has disappeared. To the mind, talk about the absolute actually *choosing* one thing over another seems to be filled with conjecture, an incongruity or contradiction. To the uninitiated, the absolute seems only choiceless. How then can the choiceless *choose?* But once we courageously walk the exquisite path, seeing each thing as it is, a form of personality that we might call *the feeling of personal intent* returns, full force.

On this path of the exquisite particular, personality makes its appearance as the face of beauty. The personality of God begins to come into focus. This divine personality helps us redefine and re-educate our own, small personality, as we include *even our own small self* in the pattern of the great *what-is.* In this way, our small version of the self begins to melt, and we see and feel the actual presence that is the personality of God, of reality, of human awakening. It is this ubiquitous, omniscient force that chooses us, that lives through us, and that we live in.

At this point, there is no difference between the absolute and the relative, and being without difference, we can say that the universe chooses us out of a conscious, directed, personal sense of compassion for us.

We arrive, and as we arrive, the compassionate particulars of personalized means arise to guide us onward. *All of this comes through our undying allegiance to seeing what-is as it is!* This is the dark bird in the morning that flies by us and reminds us to look the other way. This is the song we hear at the right moment that opens our hearts. This is you, right now, in your room reading these words. This is me, writing this, so that I can remember that the particular way the world is presented *is holy.*

We realize at this point—because of our high, clear view—that there is someone or something to pray to, not because this something or someone needs to be cajoled or convinced to help us or send succor, or even because there is a being who is eternally separate from us in any way. It is just that, as we are personal beings that the universe created in some mysterious manner, there is a mutually co-arising personal consciousness that speaks to this exquisite level of reality.

This is why Ramakrishna, even having gone through *Advaitic* (nondual) training, chose to stay a child of the

Mother Kali. This is why Ramana Maharshi rose from the basement of the temple and walked onto the mountain, where he was accessible to others for the first time. It seemed as if their great love made them do this, but the truth is that they could do no other thing: the great Love that is this universe compelled them to act in this way. It was in this way they found freedom. In each case, they chose the particular in order to find the whole world. This compassion is a particular manifestation itself and could no more change its "desire to flow to us" than we could change our skin.

In prayer, we pray to align *ourselves* so that we wake up and notice that we are held in compassion personally, as personal beings, because we are part of the entire universe and not separate in any way. Every particular aspect of this world is actually shining with this knowledge. Angels shout "Hosanna" because they are only this knowledge.

After discovering this personal compassion, we can further let down our guard and include even more of the shameful details of our life, but now in more certainty that they are part of the exquisite combination that goes into making us and that we are holy, helped by the holy, in a holy world.

Now there is no conflict between the world of mind and the features of that mind. God guides some of us to the path of oneness and some to the path of duality. But they both must end up in the same place. Whether we look at a grain of sand to find the universe or look at the nature of the cosmos to find the meaning of a grain of sand, we see that this world is enfolded in God and that God is enfolded in this world.

This is the exquisite path—the heart of nonduality— with its infinite possibilities that surrounds us every day. It is not only the angels who shout God's real name: it is the dharma of everything around us; the law that each thing reveals as it speaks its holy secret.

Here is my poem to add to old Mumon's:

> *Keeping separate*
> *in one sense,*
> *I see that the*
> *world is filled with*
> *completed things.*
> *Keeping completely separate*
> *in another sense,*
> *I see that I am*
> *a separate thing forever,*
> *with no chance ever*
> *of becoming anything else.*
> *Settled here—for better or worse,*
> *Buddha comes*
> *to love me*
> *as I am.*

THE CARE AND FEEDING
OF MY HICKORY TREE

I am so confused. You would think, after three hundred thousand years of people, people would have figured out that every bone, every nerve, every tic, every tock that we are made of, matters.

I understand it is hard. We are so...unruly. We have so much to offer but, because we are afraid, because we suffer and do not want to suffer, we cut off our own hands and then wonder why we cannot reach out our arms and feed the world. When we cut ourselves to pieces in this way, where do the orphaned pieces go? The arms we do not like, or the feet, or the fat or the thinness we are ashamed of, or the selfishness or shyness or imperiousness or arrogance?

Of course, you have to start somewhere and finding out you are not the center of the universe is a good starting place. *You are not the center of the universe!* There is only one universe that statement is true in, of course, and that is a finite one. In an infinite universe, every dot, every speck *is* the center. The difference being: in a finite universe, everyone competes to be the center. In an infinite universe, all centers are possible at once. Which brings me to another thought:

When we do not know how to heal and integrate this wonderful, miraculous sense of self-in-the-foreground, then we are forever watchful and fearful, waiting for our egocentricity to emerge once again. We are, in short, in jail, deliverance always *outside the jail cell.* Which brings me to my hickory tree.

This tree, perhaps eighty to ninety feet high, lives out in the back of my property. I should say "its property," since it was here before me and likely will be here after I am gone. It is a shagbark and its panels of uneven, unruly bark are almost on the edge of falling off, yet, they don't, and the tree stands there as it has for one hundred years, looking slightly disheveled, hairy, magnificent.

Since there has been little snow this year and since, despite that, the weeds and grasses have fallen back, I can see the deer pathways between the trees and took a walk to this tree the other day to talk to it. Usually I don't. In fact, I don't remember having ever introduced myself and, leaning into the trunk of this tree, listened. But I did it yesterday.

This hickory was an explorer and, although we are not near the sea, I could smell salt-water and follow its gaze out, far into some unknown it was leaning in toward. Its gaze was not only from its own perspective, the view from its own body, but from the four or five children it had spawned who extended this tree's vision ten, fifteen, twenty feet out, or, putting it from another angle, this hickory's vision which was its exploration itself, was enhanced by the effort of the group, standing there among deer runs and broken bottles, dumped there sometime in the last hundred years as well.

Should I subdue my ego? Should I erase it? How does an egoless boy become entangled in the magic of a hickory that is its own shining self? It seems obvious to me that to take in the world, there are my eyes, and my heart and mind, my tongue to speak praises and fears, my legs to carry me near to the tree's talking places, in short, *my*. What needs to be done then is to follow this I to its home, to return it to reason, to educate and love it so that it can be, well, the hickory inside of me, the center of the universe but one that is not superior but connected, not alone, but among.

Cloud and water monks. There is no such thing. It is an illusion. But when there is room for my own…everything…when everything inside me is allowed to be, without hatred or fear, something wonderful happens: nothing acts out and, even more important, nothing is filled up. Miraculously, there is endless room not only for my own greatness and smallness, but for every hickory and oak and pine. Every drifting cloud of smoke finds its way into my view. Every person who brings a feast or needs one, finds a home in there too.

We have not been bold enough...yet. We have waffled and cramped ourselves and our brightness. We have not discovered our own lamp. We have been afraid to be alive. So, the care and feeding of my hickory? I hear it has sweet, delicious nuts which cannot be industrialized because they cannot be counted on: some seasons, many. Other seasons, few. Sometimes for years, the hickory sits back and contemplates, explores, if you will, the sea it somehow sees despite its distance in our regular space. Me and the hickory. The hickory and me. Both old now. Both a bit bruised, but filled with hickory acorns, sweet, undependable, rare. We enjoy each other's company.

This tree teaches me how to be myself, which is to say *a self*. A self is exciting and kind. A self looks for other selves and treasures them, someone to talk to in this vast, galactic space between our birth and our death. My self and the hickory's self know the score. Billions of years for a sun, moments for a mayfly. Sometimes, two life-spans cross over each other, overlap, live at the same time before descending again into the infinite ground. I am so happy! We roam in different ways, this hickory and me, but we roam. I have never not wanted to be a person. I have never believed that we should be ego-less, whatever that means. What we should be, however, is friends. Where does your self-importance go when you are friends with everything? When you do this, you'll find your hands return, your music returns—your own music and no one else's tune—your sense of taste returns and you can taste all sorts of things, even silence.

The "care and feeding of the hickory" has been brought to you by Mr. Shulman and Mr. Hickory who have been friends for a while now. We use our egos to snuggle up to each other at night, when trees can move, and people can stop moving. Then we dream together of the sea and smell the saltwater that drifts high above everything it seems, in huge rivers in the air which bring the news from faraway.

IDENTITY

What does it mean to "celebrate identity"? And what is identity anyway?

And who does identity belong to? And why is it there? And where is it going?

For most of us, the idea of celebrating identity is tinged with the flavor of empowerment. In the seventies and especially today, with the coaching phenomena in full bloom, celebrating identity means: being more powerful; seeing yourself as having innate worth; taking yourself seriously; promoting your uniqueness; standing out; being successful.

We all know that these are good things and most of us have been through some form of empowerment work. Yet, it might be even more fruitful at this stage of our lives and spiritual growth to look at identity from another point of view entirely, one that has the root of identity as its starting point.

William Blake said:

Little Lamb who made thee
Dost thou know who made thee
Gave thee life & bid thee feed.
By the stream & o'er the mead;
Gave thee clothing of delight,
Softest clothing wooly bright;
Gave thee such a tender voice,
Making all the vales rejoice!
Little Lamb who made thee
Dost thou know who made thee

This is a great starting point: actually asking *Who made me, where did this concept of me* originate?

And Whitman:

Oh me! Oh life! of the questions of these recurring,
Of the endless trains of the faithless, of cities fill'd with
the foolish,
Of myself forever reproaching myself,
(for who more foolish than I, and who more faithless?)
Of eyes that vainly crave the light, of the objects mean,
of the struggle ever renew'd,
Of the poor results of all, of the plodding and sordid
crowds I see around me,
Of the empty and useless years of the rest, with the rest
me intertwined,
The question, O me! so sad, recurring—What good amid
these, O me, O life?

Answer.

That you are here—that life exists and identity,
That the powerful play goes on, and you may contribute
a verse.

Here Whitman gives us a hint, a pathway: to find this sort of identity, foolishness must be included in the idea of who we think ourselves to be. In other words, our identity must be taken out of the hands of the little ego and seen in its entirety, warts and all, without defensiveness. This then leads to becoming aware of "the powerful play." It is *identity* that contributes a verse.

When we are neurotic, which is to say fixated and contracted, we don't see that we are neurotic. Rather, we take our historically dependent personality as something real and valid in itself and create an identity that we believe we *own* and *are*. We are not yet capable of accepting the truth that *nothing we are* was created by us. Not our greatness or talents; our ability to be spiritual or not; our bodies, our mode of thinking, our innate genomic abilities—none of it—was self-created.

Surprisingly, instead of leaving us empty and bereft, this is a wonderful thought that brings freedom and truth, pleasure and happiness. If we take this knowledge seriously and follow it through, this understanding lets us see that every piece of manifestation, whether sentient or insentient, is a way of seeing the connection between that "vast something" and the stuff that springs from this creative flux. In other words, everything, including our own personality or identity when seen in this truthful and open way, is a gateway that lets us connect to something greater than just our individual-*only* self…if we can imagine letting go of ownership.

But somehow, we must first convince ourselves that this is true, that our most treasured keepsake—our so-called identity—does not belong to, nor was created by, us!

From the position of this new thought or understanding, it doesn't matter if you take the *personal, dualistic view*, that is, Amida (God, Reality, the Great Mother, Mind, et. al) *made all this* or the *impersonal, transcendent view*, that is, all this is the Great Formlessness in manifest form.

If you take either of these views—or some variation of your own—identity, instead of disappearing or leaving you disappointed because you don't *own yourself*, is seen as this astounding creation, no different from every rock and tree—all equally astounding. "You" now is both separate and individual and simultaneously embraces all that is. This *identity* then becomes the beginning of true celebration, and it comes with the answers to all of the questions I posed earlier.

It is from this position that we see, palpably and tangibly, that our personal identity is made of the same substance as God (or Amida, or Ultimate Reality). The very same stuff because there is no other stuff. From this position, our imperfections, no longer our identity; our talents, no longer ours; our very being, is seen to be a marvelous creation of the All. And even further, paradoxically, that this marvelous, impersonal creation, is also our truest and deepest personal self.

What is identity? The tips of the fingers of Amida as s/he dances in the void. The dewdrops that fall as drops of rain from the mouth of God; the unique, eternal and effervescent moment. What would it be like if you really said to yourself: *I only think I'm "me" when I am too close, too frozen in my own history to pull back and see the big picture.*

Who does identity belong to? You. Also, me. Also, everyone else. What would it really be like if you really said to yourself: *My very self belongs to everyone else. Not in the sense that they control me, obliterate my individuality (also God's/reality's creation!) or tell me what to do, but in the sense that somehow, somewhere, they requested my presence in the world at the same time they were present.*

Why is identity there? This is a good one. I won't spoil it by discussing it. Mums the word.

Where is identity going? It is going away. And it is coming back. Some younger person will have it soon, some kid who is not born yet or who is very small. Something will crack, something will break and out will pour light. Now I'm the vessel. One day I'll be the light.

But practice and manifestation is another, on-going story. That is something we can do together, something we can practice and practice every single moment of the day and in doing that, watch it enter our psyches and somas and take over our blind and egotistical nature, melting it, soothing it, loving it, so that we *are* empowered, unique, strong, successful, of great worth and worthy…but in an entirely different way. In a way that brings joy to everyone when you feel the joy of being you, yourself.

From this position, you can be self-concerned because, being *Self*-concerned, you are concerned for everyone else. You want their freedom and their happiness. You want their Self-concern to establish itself and spread out like a tree of life, enlivening others. What activities does this celebrated Self want to do, actually do? What will be its relationship to feeling, thought and action? What is its moment-to-moment heart, its needs and desires? When we think this way, when we do this, we can be part of the forest, a single word that contains a million beautiful trees and other beings and universes and the constant unfolding of infinite identities.

THE PLEASURES OF
THINKING

In the beginning of the long inquiry into the nature of reality, thinking is something you need to get away from. Not get *away from* exactly, but something you need to cease relating to as a trustworthy reporter as to what reality is like.

Most of us believe our thoughts. In fact, we believe our thoughts without question, without even a *second thought* about whether what we are thinking has any basis in reality. At its most basic—and its most base—this is the type of automatic thinking we all engage in when we have stereotypical prejudices. *(Those people are dirty or stupid or lazy or greedy or drunk or gamblers or insects or out to get me so I'll get them first.)* In kabbalistic thinking, we would say that this type of thinking is "thinking from the world or from the universe of *assiyah* alone." For our purposes now, *assiyah* means "the perspective where separation, the differences between things, is highlighted." This is the world of habitual response. The word *alone* as in "assiyah alone", means that instead of being integrated with other kabbalistic universes and perspectives (which through this integration unites the states of separateness and oneness), this type of perspective is split off from wholeness. Separateness as the *only* true description of what all of reality is, is completely believed. In the world of assiyah-alone, we are only separate human beings struggling for existence.

In Buddhist terms, this short-sighted belief is at the center of the primary cause of suffering: the self that thinks it exists only independently and must retain separateness in order to continue to exist. It is the heart of suffering in our psyche that both longs to belong to all of reality and shuns it for the sake of what it believes to be its survival. One of the primary ways we maintain this all-important separateness is *thinking* and taking our thoughts—which come from the separate-making part of our minds, the ego-personality—as a true picture of what reality is like. Even our images of God-consciousness or awakening or enlightenment as some *thing* separate and faraway, come from this automatic belief in thoughts that are the product of a powerful, separating part of our own minds.

Thinking about all of this, it is easy to see that using techniques that separate us from the concept of "thinking-as-truth" are quite important. Eventually, we not only begin to disengage from thinking as *content* and begin to see it as a system that has separateness as its underlying—though problematic—goal. When we do that work of stepping back from the movie of our thoughts so that we lose the sense of drama and realize we are in a theater of the mind, the power that our thoughts have to change our behavior or our mood dramatically declines. "Bad" thoughts that formerly wrecked our equilibrium are now seen to be "only thoughts." Equally, so-called "good" thoughts that raised our mood and seemed to enlighten us or make us feel better, are seen to be only thoughts as well. Good thoughts and bad thoughts: the same thing, wave up, wave down on the same ocean. As our belief in the reality of thoughts lessens, we become more and more interested in the ocean and the life below the surface or, we could say, the sea as a whole with its deepest and most surface features.

This level of spiritual work can be called the "level of insight" and this work continues for quite a while since it deals with a stratum of consciousness that is continually present: the ego's eternal questioning of how it fits into reality, of what its identity truly is.

Our unhealed egos are confused as to who they belong to: is there a me that is not the ego? Is the ego itself truly me? Or is the ego a kind of echo from the past? And if it is an echo, what was the original sound and what was its source? Was it the sound of our parents' anxiety that impressed its shape upon our ego-souls? Was it their unfulfilled longings? Their passion or lack of passion? Their own compensations and exile in the face of the difficulties of life?

Sorting all of this out is the job of insight: intelligent and neutral looking. Not only does this bring us closer to understanding our psychological patterns as we begin to see them neutrally for the first time, but it lets us peer through these patterns to the "ocean" of being, that watery ground that is *beneath* thoughts. This deep insight allows us to stop identifying with our thoughts and have deep connection to the ground of our being. We can watch ourselves negotiating with reality and seeing that effort, cast off the barnacles of bad associations, the accrued crust of culture, parents and miseducation. All this is vital. And yet.

Insight has always been very important to me. Spiritual insights are, we might say, the lifeblood of the spiritual life. We grow more intelligent through them; we open up; we learn to access our hearts. But at some point, even insights grow tedious. Or to be even more subtle, we could say that *insights become obstacles to insight.* This is true the way the body becomes an obstacle to tennis or the voice becomes an obstacle to singing. What does this mean? Well, on the crudest level, if you are still involved in the thought or sensation of singing, if you are thinking about the voice or listening to yourself from the outside as it were, you may be hired by the opera, but you'll never solo. You'll never solo because you'll never be able to reach that level where the force of life itself rides through you and the sounds you make. You'll never let go. And who is not letting go? The unhealed place in the ego that still harbors the belief that it is separate only, that it is a thing apart and must constantly look at itself in order to survive. In a sense we could say that insight itself and the desire for insight, as important as it is, is the food that continues to keep the ego quite fat, happy, and continually extending the *search* for truth instead of being *with* truth itself. At some point insight itself becomes the obstacle to the pleasures of reality.

Over the years I've spent countless hours using meditation and prayer to problem-solve and as a way of improving my condition and easing my suffering through insights into the origin of my own neuroses. But then invariably, I have been led to moments when I saw that this endless well of "stuff" would never dry up. There were always more insights to have, more pain to resolve, more history to plumb, further and further to climb. This was not a bad thing, of course, since it was also true: human folly— *my* folly—is endless and it is the endlessness that makes enlightenment more of an attitude than a thing to be achieved. I will always need to continue this sort of work. At the same time, I knew that something in my view was missing. I wasn't sure if it was the forest or the trees, but the connection between *insight* as an activity and *wholeness* was not complete. I realized I could not get to that wholeness simply through more insight alone.

I realized that any "program" of meditation was still a way of keeping the ego in an unhealed state. Unhealed because in the final analysis, the whole program of "finding out the truth" as if it was an object or place or something particular, was suspect; while it healed what was *within* the ego, it did not do the "meta-healing" of healing the ego itself. It was like always trying to find the next best medicine rather than curing the illness so that medicine was no longer necessary. It was then I discovered the pleasures of thinking.

The human mind does a whole host of things that are problematic from one perspective but acceptable from another. Thinking is an example. Thinking is what the mind does. It is not a problem any more than waves are a problem for the ocean or echoes a problem for sound. The problem is our belief in thinking as the only truth or the only way of *getting to* the truth. We are transfixed by the power of thought, trapped, in a sense, in the skull's drive-in movie theater.

The traditional way of working with this is through the program of insight, in which we neutrally observe our self thinking, thereby creating a sort of detachment, which leads to further steps. But this actually leaves a residue in that it subtly sees thinking as something that needs to be separated from; that is, it is still involved in the program of self-improvement, in separating *this place* from *that place*. While this is useful, it is only part of the solution toward liberation.

Imagine for a moment that you are meditating and that you simply *let thinking go on*. Not only that, but you let thinking go along *without either being involved in it* or *ignoring it*. Thinking simply is. It is something human beings do, something the brain does.

Now, this might sound either terribly difficult or terribly boring, but it is neither. It is the most subversive act you can imagine, and while your ego will imagine it quite clearly and even try to sabotage your attempts to do this, if you persist in refusing to be drawn into the drama of thinking and simply allow it to go on, rumbling half-heard behind a closed door, as it were, the pleasures of thinking will begin to emerge. These pleasures have little to do with the content of thought, though sometimes even that becomes—or continues—to be pleasurable. Instead, a new type of pleasure will present itself to you. We might call it the "pleasure of life," or the "way things are."

This is a level of pleasure that has no content, that has no program, that has every direction because it has no direction; that finds itself home because every direction is home. It is the pleasure a redwood feels as it grows toward the sky or that stones feel as they sit in the sun. Do not think that I am being anthropomorphic here, and that I am fantasizing that stones feel or that trees have pleasure: the type of pleasure I am talking about is not personal. It differs from purely personal pleasure in that every created thing in the universe "feels" this and—more correctly—*is this*. This is pleasure beyond the ego's ken and can only be felt in this way.

Each day when I sit in meditation, I experience the pleasure of thinking. I still genuinely need, or sometimes neurotically fall into, the need for insight. But this natural pleasure remains. It moves the world. And doing this work with our thinking aligns us with the great mystery of creation and makes life more abundant, more fertile and more of a joy. It is a practice worth trying.

CRAZY WISDOM

The first time I met someone I considered to be an enlightened being, he was very neat. His robe was neat, his bald skull shined neatly. Even his eyes looked neat. Because I was young and impressionable, I projected this neatness into every corner of his being. I assumed—more than that, I expected, insisted, and firmly believed—that his mind was neat too, and that all the suffering and neuroses that I was prey to had disappeared in this neatness, that they had been cleared away, the way shadows disappear as the sun returns from behind a cumulonimbus cloud to brighten the day.

The neatness and serenity I desired also clashed with many of the stories of masters I read about as a young spiritual student. In these stories, the actions of the master seemed crazy, without rhyme or reason and yet, somehow connected to a deeply informed and enlightened view of life. As both a teacher and a student, I desired both of these states, which seemed to be opposites.

All in all, it's hard to know the difference between craziness that is part of the neurotic state of mind and craziness that is purely—or mostly—in the service of helping others break through stultified behavior, chains made of smoke that bind every bit as effectively as metal. I've met many teachers who considered *themselves* to be enlightened and found the opposite of neatness infected their private (and sometimes public) behavior with wild egoic pieces of their personality that they considered somehow part of their wisdom and felt obligated to display before one and all who might be subjected to their teachings.

So, the question is: *What to do with craziness? Does it disappear as we go on or do we simply use it as skillful means? Is the possessor of crazy wisdom crazy like an enlightened fox or just plain crazy?*

The more I go on, the more neurotic I seem to be. In my more miserable moments I think to myself *Wow! All of this stuff seems to be twenty-five years old! So insecure, so selfish. So uptight.* In more open moments I like to think that I'm simply seeing these things within me more clearly, perhaps with utter clarity. But in my enlightened moments, I see that neither is true. What's true is *things go on.* The *who-is* of neurotic thinking, feeling and being never really goes away. Wild thoughts, aggressive thoughts. Selfish thoughts. Mean thoughts. Whatever you can think of, that part of my personality that sees the world from a separate-only perspective, the small perspective of the unhealed ego, will always—more or less—think and feel those things. What *has* changed for me, however, is the broadened spectrum available to my *who-is* and my ability to more easily use the tools of deep heart and mind to include more of the facts of the world's breadth and grandeur—a breadth and grandeur that includes my own neuroses as well. The tool that helps the *who-is* broaden its perspective, to see itself differently, is practice without a goal, unending practice. This type of practice, which is not associated only with a specific outcome, allows this craziness that is part of me to go on being in a kind of mental zoo: you can visit this zoo, view the lion if you choose, and not get eaten by the lion. In fact, from this perspective, the lion of neuroses becomes somewhat irrelevant. We no longer have to avoid the lion because in a sense, we have already been eaten by the lion: our crazy mind is the result of that feast. We are eaten but we still exist.

We might say that in usual, unhealed egoic consciousness, we are all constantly being eaten by the lion: The lion gets hungry and chews off a finger or hand. The lion gets mad and rips our belly open. Then we heal, pretend it didn't ever happen and the cycle starts again. But really, the lion and his temperament is calling the shots and every day consists to some extent of the same behavior in different forms: avoiding the lion, giving in to the lion, trying to understand the lion, surrendering to the lion. Always the lion.

But the consciousness that I'm talking about, this craziness goes on inside and in the slosh of the brain we call our mind, nothing vibrates or escapes the skull. It simply, in its small *who-is*, goes on being while something else we are that includes all of this, goes on as well. The lion is there and not there. Important and not important. Another animal in the menagerie of life.

"Crazy wisdom" is often used as an identifier for a kind of teacherly approach in certain schools of Buddhism, mostly Tibetan. Perhaps it exists is some pure form, as the art of kicking ass, the lion in controlled form. The teacher *as lion*. But mostly, I try to do my job and let the next guy worry about that special sort of craziness-as-display-of-wisdom. I wouldn't know how to do it, if it even really exists and is not also a cache of unresolved neuroses masquerading as transcendental smarts.

I once heard—I'm not sure it's true or even if this is the right person—that Rangjung Rigpe Dorje, the Sixteenth Karmapa, head of the Tibetan Kagyu Buddhist sect, said *You know, it's pretty crazy in here* pointing to his head. That, to me, is freedom. If you want to teach, *be free*. If you want to learn, *be free*. "It's pretty crazy in here" is the price of freedom, knowing that it never goes away, but that the stream clears out, never clears out, never needed to clear out and always needs to be cleared out. Nothing confusing there: just the play of the world as it is, forever and ever. This is the way to keep the world safe for enlightenment and not create any more monsters of darkness *or* of light. We don't need either. Being human, with the craziness inside, where it belongs, seems to be enough.

TRUE JOY

I would like to start our journey into the heart of true joy with a quote from *The Flower Ornament Sutra* as translated by Thomas Cleary:

> *When enlightening beings expound the teaching to sentient beings in this way, they practice it themselves increasing its benefit, not giving up ways of transcendence, fully setting out the path of transcendent practices. At this time enlightening beings give up everything external and internal without attachment to satisfy the heart of sentient beings. Thus, they can purify the transcendent practice of giving. They keep ethical precepts without attachment, forever divorcing conceit. Thus, they can purify the transcendent practice of morality. They are able to tolerate all evils with minds equanimous toward all beings without disturbance or wavering, just like the Earth, able to bear all. Thus, they can purify the transcendent practice of forbearance. They undertake all practices without laziness,*

143

never regressing in what they do, with indomitable courage
and energy, not grasping or rejecting all virtues, but able to
fulfill all aspects of knowledge. Thus, they can purify the
transcendent practice of vigor.

We don't want to mythologize our spiritual lives. We don't want to pretend to be more perfect than we are or to be more committed than we really are, more awake or more God-centered than we are.

The above passage from *The Flower Ornament Sutra*[1] asks a lot of us. In one reading, it may seem to evoke a sort of transcendent and super-human spirituality. And yet, in these lines we can find a structure and description of what it means to be a healer, both a healer of ourselves and a healer of others. In these lines we find a set of instructions on how to grow into our own fabric, into the already-present design of our souls, to begin to participate in the reason we were made and to live the life we were meant to live—to find true joy.

The first thing that this passage makes clear is that to be helpers and guides of other people, we have to be practicing ourselves. We must be involved, on a daily basis, with healing ourselves in the many ways that healing is

---

[1] *The Flower Ornament Sutra* is a very important sutra in Mahayana Buddhism, although it is known in Vajrayana circles as well.

possible. Although that is an easy thing to understand, most of the world does not act in this way. We, too, may not always act according to a simple equation: *if you truly want to help others, you need to walk the walk and not only talk the talk.* We may speak one way and then act another. Not all therapists work on their own mental health or work to have deep insights into their own psyches. Not all doctors keep to healthy precepts of living, maintaining good health. Not all politicians have their constituents' best interests at heart. Though perhaps shocking, the list goes on. However, this dictum or mantra if you will, should be first and foremost for anyone who attempts to help someone else: *unless we change we cannot help other people change.* We can also put this in a more positive way: *to the extent that we deepen and change, to that extent we can help deepen and change others.*

It is also important to understand that all of this *change* that is required of us to be helpers of one sort or another cannot be accomplished unless we develop a kind heart toward our own self. It is difficult for me to overstate that truth, that our fundamental kindness toward our own self, our imperfections and limitations, can and should be our primary resource—more than equal to any specific discipline we practice—in helping others. Though seemingly invisible, the whole enterprise of healing rests on this foundation. Kindness enlightens our disciplines and allows us to make free use of our talents in a nondual way.

The concept of nonduality is easy to understand: it acknowledges the complete connectedness of all manifestation while simultaneously honoring each particular, each of the myriad manifest things, as an abode of the holy, as another facet of the completely connected, individuated world or "reality as it is." In this way, all of existence is a single thing and this single thing contains multitudes.

This truth is always kept in mind in our school and in our practice. A Society of Souls is an intensive program in personal awakening and nondual healing. In our healings, which start with a sophisticated diagnostic process, followed by hands-on work, both healer and healee are healed. But beyond any particular approach or school, a deep, body-centered awareness of the nonduality of the world should be part of the consciousness of anyone who attempts to heal others or, by healing themselves, spread sanity in the world like a healing balm.

The above passage from the *Flower Ornament Sutra* goes on to say something even more remarkable: when enlightening beings—by the way, that is you and me—when enlightening beings practice, the practice itself is supported and its healing potential increased. The sutra doesn't look at practice as something separate from the practitioner. When the practitioner practices, the practice is changed, the practice itself evolves. Practice is not a pre-made sweater we put on, but something alive, vibrant and pulsating with change. The practice[2] –that is, any meditation from prayer to silence—*is us* and *we are it.* Practice is not a *thing* that we practice and get good at. Practice is something that meets us. We need practice and we are transformed by it, but we also transform practice. Practice is identical to who we are at the moment of practicing and is another example of nonduality in action.

This sutra also tells us something that I found remarkable and helpful. It says that enlightening beings are willing to give up everything *external* and *internal* in order to satisfy the hearts of sentient beings. Letting go of idealized thoughts about what it might take to do that, let's think about this for a moment. If you gave up everything internal and you gave up everything external, if you disengaged from the thoughts of those inner and outer worlds, what you are actually "giving up" are your *ideas* about those things.

Try this for a moment. Imagine you have a great sense of transparency in yourself so that you are not defensive, and you also have the concurrent willingness to disengage so that you can satisfy the hearts of sentient beings, which is to say, help. You give up everything internal and

---

[2] In A Society of Souls, the School for Nondual Healing and Awakening, our practice is both the many original meditations we have but also the healings we learn to give. Giving the healings to others is not simply a job or activity but a practice which activates the healing of the client as well as the healer.

everything external. What is left? Can you feel a sense of distance and separation? When enlightening beings—and again, that is you and me—give up external and internal conditions to satisfy the hearts of sentient beings, grow closer to the world. All that is left when those two things happen is openheartedness... and our skill. Openheartedness is one side of nonduality and our skill, our *particular,* is the other side. In this way, anything we do, any practice or discipline, becomes a single thing, of benefit to ourselves and others.

Enlightening beings are not altruists. Altruists still posit separation between subject and object. Enlightening beings, no longer deluded by the subject and object split, know that the world grows brighter as practice unfolds. The *Flower Ornament Sutra* explains how and why this happens: "They are able to tolerate all evils, with minds equanimous toward all beings, without disturbance or wavering, just like the earth, able to bear all—thus they can purify the transcendent practice of forbearance." Of course, knowing that I am not an archetype but a real, imperfect being, would modify the sutra's words thusly: *Even our failure, our lack of equanimity, our inability to be kind to ourselves and others, is included in this vast array of forbearance. We tolerate our own limitations, our so-called evils, simultaneously with tolerating others, and in this way our kindness is nondual and beneficial to all.*

Let's expand upon this since it is central to what real nonduality is: When the sutra says "tolerate all evils" it means that enlightening beings—again, that's you and me! —can *sustain* their consciousness *even in the face of imperfection.* To "tolerate" and "bear" may read as the call for a stiff upper lip, but it is the exact opposite—it is total flexibility within structure. That enlightening beings can tolerate all evils means that they can sustain their *continuous* consciousness in the face of imperfection. Creation has a place for everything.

Deistically and kabbalistically, we would say that this is what God did when God emanated the agencies of the world (known in kabbalistic study as the *sephirot*) a second time due to the fact that the first emanation went awry. According to this mytho-poetic vision, God had to create a container, a pattern if you will—called the Tree of Life— that could hold perfection *and* imperfection *at the same time.* The first emanation was "perfect" but not relational. The second included the failure of the first but had an increased "bandwidth" because it *was* relational. The second emanation of the sephirot included imperfection as the secret ingredient in the creation of manifestation. We could say that the "problems" in the first emanation were *included* in the second. Nothing was discarded. So, when the Tree of Life, the *Etz Chayyim*, gets re-emanated, it holds perfection and imperfection and thus, makes the real world as it is, the world God said was *ki-tov,* or "good."

This is only abstract theory until we put it into practice. How do we learn to have a type of consciousness that includes things we usually run away from, things that make us fall apart because our suffering seems to be so great that we need to disassociate from life? This is part of what spiritual work is about: learning how not to shatter in the face of life, not by "holding it together," but by being able to see wholeness *even within the shattering moment,* to see the wholeness of life, its totality, even as we *are* shattered and scattered. By practice, we slowly build up a reservoir of strength, forbearance and vigor so that we are able to see that *all of this* is what composes the present moment, that the present moment is not limited by conditions, but contains all conditions. Then we begin to entertain the fact that spiritual attainment is not about creating certain conditions but cultivating a certain attitude. We include kindness as a primary ingredient in all of this because we are undoubtedly going to fail at our task time and time again. That is the point: we are not trying to create a militaristic spirituality. We are simply just going to fall down a lot.

The truth behind all of this is the paradox of Constant Presence: how God (or reality or Buddha-nature or the real self) is "present when it is present" and "present when it is (or seems to be) not present." Even within the shattering moment, our whole consciousness remains. Even when we lose our consciousness, our consciousness remains.

According to the *Flower Ornament Sutra*, this is what the *tzaddik*[3] does—what the bodhisattva and the enlightening being does. The enlightening being doesn't just go around altruistically helping people as if people are ants and they are the gardener or ant keeper. Instead of being altruistic, the enlightening being works for himself as much as others because he or she *is* the other. The enlightening being sees the oneness and the separation simultaneously and sees both as holy. Who is there to be denied in favor of whom? When one has this understanding, the activity of enlightenment or the presence of God—however you want to put it—can go on freely, unhindered. The *tzaddik*, the bodhisattva, the healer, the helper, the lover, the mother, the father practices and, in practicing, envelops and is enveloped by the practice. That is the attitude of a healer. That is the marriage. It is like standing in the desert calling out to God as God is calling out to you, or sitting in silence doing zazen because zazen *is* enlightenment and not a way to find it.

We are always going to be challenged in trying to do these things. Laziness and all forms of resistance to life are going to rear their heads as we practice and try to "get free."

[3] The Jewish version of the bodhisattva, the wise one who works for the liberation of all.

Everything is a seed, a bit of potential around which reality organizes itself for good or ill. A thought, a belief, a practice, a lack of practice, a limiting thought or an expanding thought, each gathers energy and consciousness to itself as if it were a real thing instead of a phantasmagoria, a limited thought that makes a view or description in its own image, an editorialized view of reality that has the power to change or color our consciousness. They are seductive as well and our egos seek them out as identities until who we are is buried under misconceptions, prior conceptions, hopes and fears. We take each of these little parts of our consciousness, no matter what their evolutionary or neurotic status is, as both who we are and what reality is like. We take them to be "us" and "the world."

That these voices, these spinning things, are a part of us is not a problem. The problem is, as I said above, that we build an identity out of them and start to think that they are who and what we are. We are drawn to their self-organizing ability as they order malleable reality into a limited and specific shape, to the exclusion of a bigger vista. Our consciousness is seduced over and over again into seeing these things as independently existing beings— which is to say *real things*—instead of what they are: thoughts. And we do this to the extent that we forget who we are.

Again, if we have a truly nondual attitude, even this is not problem for us because we are a part of the lineage of those who fall down and get up, those who are perfectly-imperfect. We don't fall down so we can get up. We fall down and we get up. No fog of morality, judgment or pressure. It is simply what beings do. We fall down because it is our nature to fall down and we rise because it is our nature to rise. You don't need to be taught anything new to rise. It is your Buddha nature, your God-ing self. No teaching but this: things come and go. If we truly understand that falling and getting up are always going to happen, we can hold the whole human journey. If our focus is no longer, "Well where am I now? Am I up or am I down?" or "Who am I now, this little swirl or that one?" we can appreciate our human fullness—that bigger vista: "I am up. I am down. I am up. I am down. I am living. I am swimming in the mind stream. I am in the image of God. I am the seasons. I am the river. I am the brook. I am day and night. I am weather." Paradoxically enough, when we do this, we are free to create, to do *and* to be.

The work I developed—which grew into the school and path we call *A Society of Souls*—was designed to help us work with human suffering, our own and other people's. Our practices, whether they are specific healing modalities or meditations, are built on the foundation of letting all things in. Our diagnostic process, too detailed to go into in depth here, works exquisitely because it takes all things in. It arrives at specific healings not because it is only clear, but because it holds clarity and unclarity, revelation and boredom, insight and confusion in an equal openness and arrives at specifics as the whole is seen. We affirm our lineage as the lineage of those who fall and rise again by our practice and actions and by our inability to follow-through as well as our courage to achieve. I developed this approach to practice because I understood that very skillful means are needed to work with the difficulty of being human, which must be tremendously kind toward the practitioner as well as the client. I took myself as the laboratory and the amount of kindness I needed to grow spiritually as the example. All of this applies no matter what role you play in life.

The practices in *A Society of Souls* work together in real and elegant ways. If you take the chance to meet yourself over and over again in practice, you can discover exactly how and where all these practices fit together into a seamless whole which includes yourself and the world. If you take the chance to do these practices—or any other practices, theistic or nondual—and hold your full humanity in practice with kindness, which includes your needs and sufferings, a lot of people will be helped. It is automatic. Is this something that you are willing to discover for yourself?

Sometimes, it is not easy for us to face joy. True joy arrives when you and the practice are no longer two things but become one thing—a single thing. This *becoming one* is subtle. Do not make the mistake of thinking that *falling down* and *getting up* are two things. They are a single thing in the way a tree and sunlight must be a single thing. But they are also one because they are also two: only two things together can be in relationship. And only this level of relationship, the interconnectedness of two distinct entities, can bring true joy, the joy that is not dependent upon specific conditions but includes all conditions. Engagement with this truth is true joy. True joy is not the same thing as happiness or at least not happiness that is the polar opposite of unhappiness, though it may, from time to time, include even that. True joy is an aura of constant presence even when happiness is not present. It does not come and go when happiness leaves.

Simply put, true joy occurs when every created thing can be heard. True joy arrives when everything is allowed to have its voice, when everything can be heard and when you have devotion to allowing everything to be heard. Imagine the sound of the world if each thing has a voice. Imagine a world in which everything has a voice and you are able to hear it: the voice of sand and gravel and stones and mountains; the voice of air molecules gathered to form a cloud or a blue sky; the voice of each and every blade of grass, each root or tendril that goes into the ground and holds the plant in the earth.

Now include your own voice in the world of voices. Your voice includes your voice laughing, your voice of irritation, your voice in grief, the voice of your successes and your failures, the voice where you know how small you are, the voice where you see yourself clearly, where you are selfish, where you are cruel, where you are courageous and generous. Imagine you can hear your voice talking about the things you have yet to achieve and the capacities you have yet to develop. What is the voice that is left when you no longer have anything to say? Instead of making this a Zen koan for you to study, I'll give you the answer right now: True joy is the voice that is left in that silence. You hear all of your voices and the voice of all things in the world. And all of you listens—not just a piece of you—and as an enlightening being you don't fall apart amidst this display of voices. You see it all, you hear it all, you let it be there, and you remain faithful to it. Everything wants to return to God if you just let it. The only way to experience *this* level of joy is to experience yourself as an artist of life, practicing the art of understanding oneness and separateness on an exquisite level, moment by moment.

This work is never done. At first, this can all be quite a chore. In fact, even later it can be a chore. There will be moments where it is as natural as breathing, but there will be many times that it is not as natural. However, as you practice, even this sense of there being a "chore" is just another voice of the world, singing its slightly irritable song. The chore becomes another chirping bird, another angelic piece of grass, another irritating friend. Sometimes we blow up. Sometimes we fall apart. Sometimes we stop practicing and get somebody to call us up and remind us and we remind ourselves. All of this is going to happen if we are in the lineage of perfectly imperfect people. The message of this entire sutra said in Yiddish is the message of Reb Nachman, one of the great sages of Judaism, "Oy gevalt, never give up!"

Oh for God's sake, for the sake of God, never give up. Let nothing stop you from your true destiny, oh enlightening beings. Let nothing stop you from your true destiny, which is true joy.

With practice, you will discover that joy was not only your destiny, but your starting point; not only your goal, but your beginning.

Don't be afraid to suffer a bit. Don't be afraid to open your heart. Listen to all of the voices. Listen to the desert voice, the waterfall voice, the voices of despair, the voices of comfort, the voices of triumph, the voices of failure, the voices of stars and the void between stars. Listen to all of those voices and keep practicing until you know who it is that is speaking.

THE TERRITORY OF THE TRULY HUMAN

In a famous remark, the Indian sage Ramana Maharshi once answered a questioner who asked why he—the questioner—wasn't yet awakened by saying "Because you don't believe you are enlightened."

What Ramana was pointing to was not the idea that we should have unreasonable beliefs or egomaniacal beliefs, but that at the bottom of the barrel, the spiritual path is really about our beliefs and how they form a description of reality that either keeps us from knowledge of the divine or directs us right to it.

I would like to share a little of my journey with "beliefs" and give you an overview of the spiritual path as I have found it to be true. My hope is that even if your path is somewhat different than mine, that Ramana's words will hold true and that we can begin the descent from "beliefs" to knowledge; from ideas about the world to deep intimacy with it; from limiting concepts about ourselves and our spiritual paths to ideas that open us up to the grandeur of being entirely and completely human.

So, I'd like to draw you a map of the territory of the path as I see it. If we had enough time together, we could stop at any one of the points I'm going to make and take a week or more together to fully discuss the ideas. We could also take a lifetime together to walk the path toward liberation. But as it is, we'll be able to touch on a few very important aspects of the spiritual path and what keeps us from believing in our own hearts.

First let me say that not all beliefs are created equal. Some beliefs, because they are not about superficial things, but about fundamental aspects of reality such as suffering, imperfection, love, God, awakening, enlightenment and so on, are so ingrained in our DNA, so close to the bone, that they have a profound effect upon us and the world. This level of beliefs—powerful, but often hidden—are the type of beliefs we need to explore together. Second, I'd like to make the point that everyone reading this is on a spiritual path whether you consciously acknowledge it or not. The fact is: the entire content of every spiritual path is simply the content of our day-to-day life. There is no other content to the spiritual path but this life itself. The spiritual path is every moment of our life. So, just by the act of being alive, we are all constantly dealing with all of the content of the so-called spiritual life, but in an unnamed way, on a day-by-day basis.

We are all practicing life; getting entangled in life; seeing our way through life; learning to explore and live life. We don't need to sit a certain way or wear some special article of clothing to be spiritual. Life presents us with its full content at every moment.

At the same time, there are people who have decided to be consciously aware of these lessons life presents and who have therefore decided to follow a method that speeds up their interactions with life, that purposely invites life's lessons in so that they can be explored more deeply and perhaps even more quickly. The study of Kabbalah or the study of Buddhist koans or the practice of meditation or prayer, are all ways of studying who we are in relationship to life; to study our life in life.

Spiritual paths are like searchlights that illuminate the path of life, the territory we are actually walking. They help us see what we are trying to express by being alive.

So, what is this territory? We could express this landscape by putting it in the form of a question: how do we become fully human? We could also say, what is it like to become fully human and how do we actually do it? And also: can it be done by me?

Awakening, God-realization, enlightenment—whatever we call it—without all the romance comes down to this: awakening = being fully human. It is very important that we ask these simple but profound questions, because only in that way can we see if the answers we have found lead us onward toward our goal or actually block us from what we seek. So, to deepen our journey, we need to begin to make an assessment of what we believe and what the implications are of these beliefs because our beliefs change our lives.

So:

- Do they bring us closer to people or push people farther away from us?
- Do they make us happier and create in us a willingness to allow other people to be happy as well?
- Do they help us recognize the tentative hold we have on this planet and do these beliefs suggest a course of action?

Kabbalah without this practical result is interesting but of little consequence. Buddhism without connection to other people is a lonely meal at a table for one. The same is true of any other path based on any other religion.

Let me be very direct about this important issue: it is not just "beliefs" in general, but our unexplored beliefs that stand in the way of our being able to experience God as a palpable and constant presence—to use deistic language— or the state of intimacy with reality, to put it another way.

We often don't know why we have certain beliefs or even where they came from. In fact, most of us are unconscious about our deepest beliefs about life and the spiritual path, beliefs so deep they lie hidden and invisible at the bottom of our minds. We don't even know that some of these beliefs we hold about spirituality actually limit our freedom and awareness and are thus the opposite of what we really want. In this sense, we are still asleep. True spiritual learning is about waking up to what we believe to be true so that we can see these beliefs in the light of day and test whether they extend or limit our freedom. We cannot see the bars of the jail cell we keep ourselves in unless we open our eyes.

The wonderful thing is the more we wake up to what we believe, the more we come out of fantasy about who we are and what life is, the more we step out of this jail. So, it is not so much a matter of learning about the jail cell, feeling its dimensions, looking at its furnishings and so forth. It is about discovering the beliefs we hold that not only keep us in this cell, but which make us believe there is a jail cell there to begin with! When we do this, even before we correct or change our beliefs, when we see the "what-is" of our life, we begin to find God right where we are. The secret is that the divine is always close at hand.

So, I would like to alert you to three fundamental beliefs that often create misunderstanding of what spiritual awakening actually is: getting rid of or transcending the ego, the truth of suffering, and imperfection.

The Ego

One of the beliefs we all have is that to make progress on the spiritual path, we have to do something to our ego/personalities. Usually, the thought is that we need to transcend our ego or to see it as an illusion in some way. In either case, the ego is something to be gotten rid of.

In A Society of Souls, our school of awakening and healing, we are careful to make a distinction between the healing ego and the un-healed ego. Our hope is to heal the ego and not do more violence to our soul by trying to kill something that holds within it the great promise of liberation, something that, in its essence, is the moment of liberation itself. Please understand that I am saying that the personal ego—when healing and understood—is the moment of liberation itself because the healing ego is no longer entranced in making up stories about itself and in this way separating itself from life. Instead, the healing personal, egoic self is in intimate contact with life. But through misunderstanding and miseducation, the healthy ego's importance in creating and sustaining human wholeness has been denied. The consequence of doing this is to enter a spiritualized fantasyland where who we are as separate and whole individuals is erased in favor of some foggy notion of goodness. We don't tell a mountain not to be a mountain, but we constantly tell ourselves not to be people. People—individuals—only exist because of and with—an ego. There is no person without an ego, though there can be a person with a healing ego.

Think of this for a moment: your body is made of billions upon billions of bacteria. Pieces of the earliest forms of life on this planet still exist within your cells as mitochondria. Your brain is made of billions of nerve cells connected in trillions of ways. Your DNA is made from proteins; these proteins then form organs, these organs, systems, these systems a functioning body.

The miracle is: this bag of historical protoplasm thinks it is a "somebody." It somehow holds a steady point of view. It creates a unified identity it calls "a person."

If there is such a thing as blasphemy for a Buddhist, the idea of an essential, steady self, that has its own reality, is it. Much of the work of meditation is to begin to see through this so-called self; to see, as Buddha did, the inherent "emptiness" of the personal self, the fact that there is no *there* there! This is very important since many psychological diseases come along with this miracle of self. For example: my self is more important than your self. And yet, we must ask ourselves if this is the whole picture.

Another belief, a little more abstract, but just as important is: this universe is too big, to real, too intense for my self to take in. I need to cut it into pieces; I need to make it smaller than it is in order to feel safe. And I need to cut any other lively beings down to size too, so they won't threaten my sense of safety.

Here's another one: I will die and therefore I will not exist since I am only a separate self.

The list goes on.

But the truth as I see it is this: this self is a miracle, and the healing self is that miracle expressed. In other words, the end result of healing the wounded, historical, personal self is that the Self and self, big "S" and little "s," exist together as one thing when the personality is healed through the hard work of psychological and spiritual inquiry. Then the belief that our "small self" and our "big Self" are somehow two different things is no longer true. Please pay attention to this statement! We begin relying on the truth that essentially this thing—the S(s)elf—that seemed to be divided in two, is actually one shining thing. And this is not illusion because we have done the hard spiritual and psychological work to begin to heal both the split and the belief.

The ego is not bad in any way. It is only an aid to receiving God or reality when it is healthy or an obstacle to receiving these same things when it is unhealed. And even in its unhealed state, this ego still has that spark within it that constantly says There must be a better way: Find it! It urges us onward. The personal self is the temple of awakening and enlightenment. It is God's tent, too. And though filled with distortions, it is filled with the voice of freedom, no matter how faint and far away.

Try this for a moment:

Just close your eyes for a moment and listen for that faraway, small voice. It is either saying something like, I understand what this fellow is saying or I'm not sure what he is saying. Your inner voice may be also saying other things, making judgments, congratulating you or whatever. A constant stream of dialogue. In either way—positive or negative—what is speaking is that part of your psyche that is trying to find liberation or freedom. If you forget about the specific content of this voice's message for a moment, just try substituting these words:

My self is trying to find a way to understand. My self is trying to lead me toward wholeness. My self is trying to find a way to understand. My self is trying to lead me to wholeness.

The ego sometimes drives us crazy with its unreasonable demands, but at the bottom of it all, it is just trying to help us.

Please take a moment and think of your ego in these two ways:

- as a bothersome thing that stands in your way and only causes you grief,

and then

- as a potential ally and vehicle for change and exploration that is trying to lead you home as best it can.

This second statement is the deepest message of the ego. The problem is, however, that most people do not listen to their real, personal selves. Instead, they listen—unconsciously—to someone else's personal self. They have taken on someone else's world view, limited view, ideas, beliefs, not as tools to explore reality and the divine, but as ways to limit it. This limits life itself. And though this voice, even when we hear our own, can be problematical and needs healing itself, we should not ignore the fundamental desire our ego personality is trying to communicate as best it can.

The point is not to imagine some fantasy state of egolessness, but to see who we are in every moment, no matter what it looks like to our frightened, self-judging self. To see how, bit by bit, the healing personal self is automatically generous; to see how we automatically feel blessed when a wounded part of our self is brought back into the family of who we are, so that our wholeness becomes a real and manifest thing. That we are glad to be ourselves. That being our self is no longer a self-centered affair but something so large it is practically unspeakable.

Spiritual work is always work on and with the ego. Our whole spiritual journey is about healing our unhealed egos which do not know how to partake of the world as it is. The world is not safe because people do not do this sort of thing and instead believe the propaganda their unhealed egos broadcast to them day and night, that survival requires the death of otherness; that freedom means supremacy and that only the conqueror is free. All of the messages of the unhealed ego are really cries for help from the ego in the only language it knows: resistance, fear, pride, self-will and pain. Our job as spiritual seekers is to listen carefully for the message underneath so that we can give this ego what it truly wants: to be free; to be love itself; to be kind. To be wise. To be unshackled. To walk upright with dignity. To help. To trust life. Our small self does not need to be violated or killed for this to happen. It simply needs to find a home.

Eventually, we begin to experience a state of enjoyment in this process of awakening or God-realizing. This type of enjoyment has no opposite because it embraces all of what-is, even the un-healed and separate-only parts of our being. It is then we begin to understand the constant presence of God.

The Truth of Suffering

What other beliefs do we have that stand in the way of our attainment of our true humanity, our true enlightenment and liberation? For many years I thought that enlightenment or awakening or being with God meant the end of human suffering, specifically, that it meant the end of my suffering.

Because many of us may share this belief, let me be quite clear: enlightenment or awakening or God-surrender does not mean the end of suffering. By virtue of having a separate self and a separate body and family and friends and a world, all of which are tender and mortal, we are all destined to suffer. However, because we believe we should not suffer—that something, like God or enlightenment, should save us completely from suffering—we actually suffer more, adding to the suffering we cannot avoid as human beings.

If we call this suffering that we all hold in common primary suffering, you might say that we all create secondary suffering in an attempt to escape this primary condition.

We elaborate upon our suffering, expanding it, and creating new, more "desirable" suffering—we believe—because it seems to substitute what seems to be smaller problems for the fundamental problems of life and death.

Here is a simple example: Let's say that I believe—as I once did—that life itself should only contain what I consider "light," and that when difficulty or darkness comes, I need to avoid it like the plague. Perhaps I create more suffering by using certain drugs or alcohol to re-enforce this sense of light or to eliminate my fear of difficulty and darkness. The drug used in this case is a secondary suffering, a pain preferred to looking at the truth of life. Or let's say I'm afraid to experience grief—which is a fundamental part of life—so I get overactive. Eventually this over-activity wears me down and I begin to get sick. All of this suffering is secondary to the desire to avoid the original, existential pain of grief.

It is hard work to get back to the original, existential suffering. That is why the Buddha put the truth of the existence of suffering as his first Noble Truth. He was asking us to come out of fantasy and to notice what is true about life.

But when we do come out of fantasy, and when we can bear to feel this truth, a paradoxical thing happens: we find ourselves in God's house; we find ourselves in our true nature; we find ourselves awakening. Primary suffering—unlike secondary suffering—always has within it a sense of life. It is life-enhancing, even when it is about our mortality or loss. And returning to the true condition of life, rather than resisting it, sets us free.

This existential suffering which we all hold in common is not an impediment to awakening, it is the fundamental tool of enlightenment and God surrender. Koan study, meditation, prayer, are all practices that bring us out of our secondary suffering so that we can see life as it is. Being born, aging, illness and death are part of life no man or woman can avoid. But when seen without the aura of secondary suffering, they lead to greater awakening, greater God-realization and greater happiness, all of this in a still imperfect world.

Imperfection

This brings me to the final belief I'd like to examine with you: imperfection.

Imperfection is the name of the game. As long as we are attached to some idea of perfection, we are doomed to be in hell part time and heaven part time as the unhealed ego likes—or does not like—what is going on within it and around it. Imperfection is the name the small, separate-only egoic self gives to the ebb and flow of reality as it is perceived by our sense organs, brain and consciousness.

In the kabbalistic story of creation, God needed to emanate manifest creation two times because there was an imperfect moment in the first emanation. In this story, the first time God emanated the sephirot[4] everything went well until a certain point. Then things went awry for many reasons and the emanation of the Tree of Life could not continue as it was. A new, second emanation needed to happen in which the process could continue again from where it broke off, in a new way. This moment of imperfection is very, very important in kabbalistic understanding.

Some commentators ignore that moment of imperfection, when the first gateways to the divine went awry and need to be "corrected." They assign blame for this imperfection to human beings and see the path as being one by which imperfection is banished into perfection again. But by looking at this story in this way, they miss the fact that the "purpose" of the failure of the first emanation and the need for a second emanation was to incorporate the idea of imperfection deeply into the manifest world and, by extension, into us as well. It seems that imperfection is somehow a necessary part of manifestation.

We could say that by having two emanations, the prime mover of the universe was creating a relationship with imperfection itself. God, as the metaphor for this prime

---

[4] Briefly, we could say that the *sephirot* are levels or "shapes" of revelation that are the fundamental pathways for all the dimensionality and relational connectivity of the created world. In traditional Kabbalah, these are emanations of the divine. They are expressed in the matrix kabbalists call the Tree of life or the *Etz Chayyim*.

mover, must be able to have a relationship with all conditions of reality. This was the way the perfect and imperfect could be held together, with no duality at all, and it gives us a model of how to hold imperfection in our own lives, not in opposition but as united partners in the constant act of creation.

Finally, we need to understand what it is in all of us that makes us want to go on this journey, this hard journey from a fragmentary existence to wholeness; from forgetting to remembering who we actually are.

Love

From my perspective, love is a force that is embedded in the very reason for material existence, that is expressed in the very fact that atoms of matter cling together to form elements, molecules, stars, proteins, DNA and us; that we have mouths to speak and ears to listen. It is something we see more and more clearly as our egos heal, until it is completely apparent, and we wonder why we didn't see it all along. It is the fact that material existence—ourselves and the world—are all essentially made of love.

That is what the path is for—whatever we call our particular path—to see and make real this power. To be motivated by it. To move forward through our lives knowing that the movement, our lives and the world are all expressing this fundamental thing.

The only reason that this journey through misconception to light is possible is that no matter what path you choose, if it is a true path, if it is a path that will take you to the heart of your hope and let you see the world and yourself as they essentially are, and if it will liberate you from the bondage of the past, it will do so because it is a path that takes note of love, a path whose end result is to return to love.

Finally, at the beginning and at the end, love is all there is. All of the hard work and thinking about these things comes down to learning how to be more open-hearted in a real way. Love cannot be split into love for others as opposed to love of self. To love one side and not the other is not love: it is sentimentality. Love cannot be torn asunder in that way. This form of love always includes the lover and the beloved. It cannot debase one or the other and still be love.

This form of love is not exactly a feeling in our hearts but rather a way of living. It appears gradually and automatically as the ego resumes its non-neurotic state. And as we do this, we wake up. There is no other name for it. We wake up to God, to God-consciousness, to self-realization, to our truest nature, our Buddha-nature, whatever we choose to call it. And we don't wake up as a one-time experience. We begin to have a relationship to waking up to things as they are over and over again, moment by moment. And in this waking up, we see more and more clearly both the pain of the world, the suffering of the world and the inherent, essential beauty the manifest world is; a quivering, powerful and delicate thing. We begin to understand that God, awakening, enlightenment, whatever, along with being truth, is beauty as well. Once you touch this, even if it is only for a few moments, it enlivens your soul and helps you discover your commitment to walking the path of the spirit, your commitment to the real. And you discover this not because this commitment is something you add on to who you are. You discover that fundamentally, you are nothing but this commitment and that you are shimmering like everything else in creation, walking toward God even as you are in God, awakening because being awake is your nature and was so from the very beginning.

OWNING THE SELF

Many years ago, I visited a Zen Center to do an evening meditation. The young monk who gave a talk pointed to a sculpture in the shape of a wheel. *Every person is on the top of the world,* he said and pointed with his fan to the top of the wheel. *No matter where you are, you are on the top!*

This statement can be very confusing to us because, for the most part, people do not associate "being in the real self" with being on top of anything. In fact, it is quite the opposite. Most of us think that if we are living our true selves, we will be easy-going, and have a generally non-egoic attitude toward life. Our sense of preference will diminish, for example. We will be like a monk with his begging bowl: part of enlightenment or awakening will be eating whatever is put in the bowl. In fact, there are stories in some sutras and Zen stories about how unconcerned some practitioners have been with what was placed in their bowl, eating scraps of food and worm-eaten food with equal gratefulness.

I remember reading a story about a Zen master's trip over on a boat from Japan to San Francisco. He was remembered as sitting in deep zazen on the upper deck unconcerned that flies were biting him. Though these stories do have much to recommend them, they are also misleading and equate a certain kind of *selflessness* with enlightenment. But enlightenment is not about being selfless: it is about owning the self.

There is a tale told about how Ramana Maharshi once broke his collarbone as he tried to intervene between a monkey who was grabbing food from Ramana's favorite squirrel. Ramana fell and the consequence was a broken collarbone. What does this tell us about the self? Ramana, for example, had many clear-cut preferences. He liked a particular cow, a special squirrel. He liked to drink coffee in the morning. He liked to read the news. At the same time, in his younger days—before, in my estimation, his insight-experience developed into enlightenment—he sat with insects running all over his thighs, his particular trance of immersion in a state of no-preference unbroken.

Does the enlightened self have preferences? Does someone who surrenders their life to God still have a personal life?

The answer from my perspective is that unawakened people *have a self*. Enlightened people *use the self*.

When we *have* a self, that is, pinned down to being *only* a self as our sole identity, then paradoxically enough, there is another, imagined self with which we compare ourselves and which we judge ourselves against. Self, held in this bounded way, begets this other fantasy self we measure ourselves against. We are not completely whole. In this case, preferences are a way of reinforcing our identity. In a real sense, preferences *are* our identity in this situation. That is how we know who we are. *Using* the self, on the other hand, is a different state of affairs. Here we are *using* a tool, a tool which can have preferences or not. Identity *per se* does not come into the picture.

This division between these two types of selves or even the existence of them, is not so much of a problem, but being *unconscious* of these two versions of the self, one which we are identified with and one which is simply used, is. Being *unconscious* of this predicament leads us to continue to create false selves in an effort to discover—through comparison—some behavior that will save us from the suffering of being split in two.

In a way, maintaining the unconscious split between the selves is a way of remaining in the known. There is always something there, a sense of who we are, a kind of background murmur that is constantly checking in with us to see how we are doing. It is a kind of neurotic mountain guide who keeps guiding you after you've come home, when you are eating dinner, when you talk with friends and when you go to sleep.

Using the self, on the other hand, brings us directly into the unknowns of life. Consider for a moment that you do not constantly tell yourself how to pick up a glass of water. If your arm is not injured, you simply *use* the arm for the action you require. If your arm *is* injured, the story is different. Then you need to think about how you will use your arm and use it carefully.

It is the same with the ego. I say "the ego," because there is no enlightenment *without* the ego. *It is the ego that gets enlightened!*

When the ego is ill, that is to say neurotic, for most of us, we do not so much *use* the ego as the ego *uses us.* This means that the ego, in its unhealed state, uses the mental facility of comparative intelligence to check out whether it is OK. It looks at our actions, our feelings, our thoughts, our bodies, our attainments and our failures, to see if it will continue to survive in a state it recognizes as itself.

When we *use* the ego, on the other hand, we use it to make decisions (for example, liking the squirrel more than the monkey's behavior at the moment), or understanding you actually *are* at the top of the world in that there is no one like you in the entire universe, that when you stand on your legs, a fully alive being using all of his or her accoutrements, you give the lion's roar of an awakened being simply by being yourself.

Since my idea of awakening is not a militaristic one, one in which there is some sort of constancy that never ever falters, what do we then do with the fact that for most of us sometimes we will use the ego and sometimes the ego will use us? What do we do with our imperfect humanity?

Remember, the unhealed ego likes nothing better than to think of some state in which attainment is constant, unvarying, without defect or change. This is simply the unhealed ego's dream of nirvana.

The healed ego on the other hand knows what it is like to fail and has made failure a friend. It is closer to its humanity and further from an idealization—or even *idolization*—of what surrender to the real is about. We could say that the healed ego's fearlessness, its ability to "be on top of the world," extends even to its faults and it sees benefit, in fact benediction, in the inelegance of the human way, the curvilinear way, the way that shifts from winter to spring, that falls apart and comes back together.

Owning the self means owning *all* of the self. It is not a capitalistic stance. It is not self-abnegating. It stands where it is, or we could say it stands where is *is*.

Awakening is both universal *and* particular. It is as open as the skies and only as big as a body. In other words, there is no limit to the openness of awakening since it is not frightened by the large or the small.

IT'S DIVINE KNOWING YOU: THE SPIRITUAL MEANING OF COMMUNITY

Sangha. Congregation. Havurah. Tribe: It has been consistent throughout recorded history that a vital component of the personal spiritual journey has been its connection to the group, the relationship of the solitary seeker to his or her brothers and sisters on the path.

On the most obvious level, it's easy to understand: We want people to talk to; we want to share our experiences; we want support and love from like-minded people as we take the sometimes-difficult journey of awakening to our true nature, of finding God. But hidden under these formative ideas lies a dynamic spiritual system without which, though often not overtly stated, personal spiritual progress—or complete spiritual progress—could not be accomplished. In other words, spiritual community exists not only to support us and make things easier, but to challenge us, to push us forward, and to help us see one of the primary truths of reality. Let's talk about a few of them.

Community as Sandpaper

Everyone has a personality, god help us. Sometimes we like their personality and sometimes we don't. Sometimes we *really don't.* And yet, since we have actually *chosen* this community, unlike the community of our families which we were born into, it's difficult to pick and choose. Everyone is there for the purpose of spiritual growth and we come to understand at a certain point that our preference has nothing to do with who gets to stay part of the community and who's asked to leave. It's not up to us.

So, we are left to our own devices and, because we are dedicated seekers, we are forced to begin looking inward at our own preferences rather than outward at our judgments and beliefs.

A good spiritual community is one that understands from the very beginning that there will always be conflicts within a community and that two things must happen. The first is that each person is completely, one-hundred percent responsible for their own response; even if another person has done something incorrect or downright wrong, *our response* is *our responsibility*. The second is that things must always be worked out and not papered over in the false hope of having a "happy home."

Spiritual work is not about having a happy home. The Buddha said that *Buddhas are those beings who are greatly enlightened about their delusions*. This means that spiritual work is about uncovering, seeing, accepting, working with and through our own imperfections. Not the imperfections of others: that's *their* one hundred percent!

So, the community setting is vital to our own growth because it causes friction. This is not the failure of community. The failure occurs if we don't take personal responsibility and, at the same time, have an avenue within the community for the working through of human troubles.

Eventually, we become grateful for the sandpaper of community. We begin to ride more lightly and begin seeing that all of us, ourselves included, get on someone else's nerves, and that it is our nerves that need to be a little more seasoned, a little more loose in the saddle, a little more open to the vagaries of human conduct; we understand that we are all imperfect beings and will forever need to work things through with the world around us.

Community as Relationship

A corollary to community as sandpaper is community as the truth of relationship. If we look at the world with open eyes, with fearless eyes freed from limiting and unexamined beliefs, we see that the world is constantly in relationship. If we are really brave, we understand that relationship comes in all shapes and sizes, from the warmest love to the coldest fury: all the possibilities of how we connect are on the continuum of relationship. From the smallest microbes to the largest galaxies, everything is in collision and needs this collision of desires and needs and material in order to exist.

While we may fantasize that in the world of spirit there is room for everything with no chance of conflict, once out of the world of spirit and in the material plane, it's as if there isn't enough room for everything. In fact, if we look at anything in this world closely enough, we see that one thing is constantly eating another thing in order to survive. Some people think it better to eat things like vegetables rather than animals, but the fact remains that one thing must die in order for another to live. Despite all this evidence, human beings have a thought that there is such a thing as relationship that does not contain strife. In this vision, there is no conflict. We are all in Eden or Heaven and the lion has decided to lie down with the lamb. This is not possible of course. The only way the lion and the lamb lie down together is if the lamb is going to be lunch. We have to shut our eyes very tightly not to see that conflict is fundamental to life and not only that: that it is relationship that is fundamental and basic.

Once we understand this and can begin to accept it, we can move out of fantasy and examine the fact that "community," that is, other people engaged in the same pursuit we are engaged in, is actually an out-picturing of a basic truth of existence: we are all one. In this vision, oneness does not mean we are all the same: this is a vast Oneness that includes difference and difference is the name of community. At some point, instead of irritating us, differences between ourselves and others become a cause for celebration. This one is good at singing. This one is not. This one can run fast. This one is slow. This one is good at helping others. This one likes to keep to herself.

Once our ego-centric preferences are worn down by the sandpaper aspect of community we get to see the glory of difference, the enriching quality of the unusual, the deeper meaning of how abundance manifests on our plane of existence through the garden of human variation.

The Poor in Spirit

Years ago, I was part of a spiritual community that followed a certain set of teachings. There were evening meetings, weekend workshops and a center where we stayed overnight (and some people lived). There was one fellow who, while living at the residence, did not attend any of the meetings or workshops. He didn't even eat with the rest of us but was always busy cooking his food—he only ate beans and rice and tofu—for his special diet. None of us actually ever knew if he followed the teachings or how he became part of the community. Some people wanted to ask him to leave. I always thought he was quite valuable to have around.

Jesus said that the poor in spirit are always with us. I love this statement. Let me quote a little Zen story to illustrate how I understand this statement:

A young monk goes to his teacher and says, *What is the meaning of the Patriarch's coming from the West?*

Now, this question about the Patriarch refers to the founder of Ch'an (which later became Zen), Bodhidharma, and why he came from India to China, bringing Zen with him. In other words, in the Japanese tradition, this is shorthand for, *What's it all about? Why meditate? Why this entire enterprise of trying to get free?*

The Master answers: *To grow weary and tired.*

The master could have said: *To become poor in spirit.* Jesus' statement as reported in Mathew goes on to say that the poor in spirit will inherit the Kingdom of Heaven. Why is this? My understanding is this: only as we drop our concepts do we see the light of the world. Or put more simply: only as we drop our preconceived beliefs, our prejudices, do we wake up and see what is actually in front of us. This is the whole point of spiritual attainment: to actually see what is in front of us!

For me, asking this person to leave was vastly premature: his presence could actually foster great spiritual growth for us all. If we were brave enough, we could actually listen to many of our cherished—but unfounded— beliefs falling like so many trees in the forest: *He's weird. Ka-boom! He's not as sophisticated: Ka-boom! He makes me feel afraid. Ka-boom! I don't understand him: Ka-boom!* And so on.

My effort in recent years has been to become poor in spirit: less filled with myself and more filled with the divine. It's not that everything is not divine. We just don't see how that can actually be until we put down the burdens—long held! —of our limiting and hidden assumptions about what is valuable and what is not.

Community as Sanctuary

Finally, we come to the idea of safety, of a place we can come home to. It is impossible to take this ride alone. Yes, perhaps for a while, but at some point, friends are the only traveling companions along any path of freedom. But this freedom cannot come if it is still based on everything I've said above. In other words, real sanctuary appears when we allow difference, when there is room for conflict, when we take total responsibility for everything we feel and stop believing that others cause us to feel a certain way. As that is accomplished, or at least as that is held out as a way to travel along the spiritual road, then community becomes a true place of refuge, a place we can be ourselves since no one is pressuring us to be like them. A place where getting into trouble is expected and worked through; a place we don't come to to be perfect but a place we come to grow into our imperfect, heart-felt and holy humanity. That's the community for me.

INTIMACY:
THE HEART OF HEALING

I'd like to begin with a focus on obstacles to intimacy. By saying "obstacles to intimacy" I am implying that intimacy is our natural state, and that there are obstacles to this natural state. I believe this to be true.

When we are babies, although our full intelligence has not yet manifested itself, certain aspects of our innate intelligence are in full bloom. For example, as babies we are intimate with everything: breast, bottle, milk, water, poop, pee, rocks, pebbles, dirt, food, everything. In fact, one of the tasks mom and dad have to do is to teach the young one to separate what is *good* and what is *bad*.

When we do this teaching, we are actually involving ourselves in the development of the child's memory function. This important and inevitable teaching—and our part in creating a being who knows *before, now,* and *after*—has far reaching consequences. It brings us into the stream of time in a way that connects the lessons of the past with what we can expect in the future.

Even though this is quite important, it too has the consequence of conditioning us to see things in the present as an echo of some past experience. Again, this is quite positive, but also has consequences, one of which is of not letting us see things as they are and respond to things freshly and with gusto, with a different sort of intelligence that we might call "original intelligence in the now." We could also call it the intelligence of *intimacy*.

So, this mental conditioning, involving memory and the egoic function—which exists because it is the carrier of memory—reappears holographically throughout our lives, in various guises and doing various jobs. We need to look at how it reappears in our role as healers or as promoters of healing principles in other arenas of life and work.

Healers and helpers in our tradition can be seen as having two conflicting jobs. This is true because Nondual Kabbalistic Healing springs from a unitive view of what true healing is. For example, the Diagnostic Process[5] in NKH

---

[5] The Diagnostic Process is a method—or really a vehicle—that students of Nondual Kabbalistic Healing use to decide which of the many healings they know is the right one for the person they are working with. Unlike characterological approaches—or even psychological ones—the DP is an art form that does not attempt to narrow down the myriad of possibilities in order to find the right diagnosis and therefore the correct approach for the person. Instead, by a process that includes all the opposites the healer finds in the

does not depend solely upon intuition as opposed to memory, being as opposed to doing, and so on. In other words, the diagnostic process, for those who have learned it and for those who will, includes all the opposites and rides the wave that connects all opposites to find the right healing or action for the moment at hand.

So, in NKH healing, our relationship to opposites is – unusually—inclusive.

For example:

One job that presents itself is to heal, to make whole, to change and modify, to fix and to cure. In other words, whether it is our unhealed ego that wants this or some

---

interaction, the correct healing is found not by objectifying the client but by creating a form of intimacy that comes from the totality of the interaction between the healer and the client. This means that all the seeming opposites one encounters on this journey are not only accepted as part of the process but are vital to it. In this way, clarity and confusion, excitement and boredom, being lost and being found, as examples, form a perspective of the client that is deeply enriched in all dimensions rather than one that is concentrated on the pathological issues alone. This radical inclusion even includes the healer's own transference, which the healer has learned to accept through a positive process we call riding the wave of transference, which recognizes the precious possibilities inherent in the rectified form of this non-verbal communication. In this way, all is information, and intimacy is established by the broadening of contact with all aspects of the client and healer themselves rather than a characterological narrowing down. The result is the paradoxical movement toward open and nonjudgmental contact, along with the specificity of just the right healing for that occasion.

transcendent feature of our consciousness, we cannot avoid this impulse within us.

The second job, a sort of skillful means, is to see things as they are. We understand this as the primary way we can begin helping. If we don't see things as they are, we cannot exact the right medicine. If we cannot bear to leave things as they are, our trust in the universe never becomes deep enough to change our lives.

Being and doing. See things as they are without the urgency to change them versus change them, bring more peace, health and wholeness.

What I would like to make clear is that *intimacy* is the transcendent tool that allows us to reconcile and reunite these two seemingly opposed streams in our effort to help others.

Intimacy is called transcendent because it is not limited or thwarted by opposites, but like the heart, which can hold opposites and contradictions easily, intimacy holds all of what is close to it.

Because intimacy allows us to be so close to everything, it is the ultimate protection and brings about the ultimate healing. Unlike gullibility, which is wishy-washy and has no bones or structure, intimacy has great intelligence and shape.

In fact, we could use many opposite words to describe true intimacy: It is open and cautious. It is naïve and realistic. It is passionate and it is detached. All of these qualities go into making intimacy what it truly is.

Intimacy can be intimate because it is without territory to defend. It is not encased in the jail of *either/or*.

It is also true that intimacy is not the product of the personal self *only*. It cannot be achieved by *choosing* to be intimate but arises out of an experience that includes the personal self that is ready to experience it but is simultaneously beyond the purely personal self.

Friendship is a personal product. But intimacy has an element of the transpersonal and transcendent in it. It is not centered around the protection of the personal self, but its enlightenment and healing. This means it allows the shape of the personal self to morph and change, something the unhealed ego, which is not the vehicle for true intimacy, cannot do.

It understands that true healing starts with being connected to everything, to having the eyes of the body, mind and spirit open. The body of intimacy is the open heart, both personal and transcendent. It is both personal, as in a sense of feeling, and impersonal, which not only includes feeling, but intelligence as well.

The mind of intimacy is an opened mind. An open mind is courageous enough to see *what is* instead of seeing the echo of the past in the present moment. In other words, it doesn't only rely on memory to explain what is happening in the present moment but is willing to meet what is in front of it without conceptualization and limitation.

When we are intimate, we know what to defend against or reject and what to accept; we have a clear mind and a clear mind is an intimate mind.

How does this play out in the very concept of "healing"? What are the assumptions we make about healing that actually limit what healing is and could be? The main item I want to focus on here is the concept of *difference* and how it encourages or discourages intimacy.

As healers of any sort, we always run the risk of pathologizing our clients. Our client walks into our practice room and we say mentally to ourselves: *what's wrong?* Or even *how can I help this person?* From the point of view I am presenting, which is a very advanced notion, either comment is suspect!

We habitually do this for two reasons: Sometimes it is in our job description! We are presented not with the whole person, but with the part in trouble and we have been trained to respond only to the part in trouble. An emergency medical worker is a pure example of this. You don't want to be treated in an emergency situation by someone who is going to withhold treatment while they ponder the existential reasons for your predicament!

All of us find ourselves in situations that call for this type of thinking. But I am not so much interested in these conditions: they are pretty straightforward.

More subtle are those moments that we *choose*—usually unconsciously—to *not* see reality and to not see what I am calling *difference*.

In the beginning of our adventure as healers, and in the beginning of our adventure as spiritual explorers, we tend to, and *need* to clearly see the negative patterns in our lives and work to correct them. In A Society of Souls our main tool for doing this is to bring things to consciousness and then hold them in a form of kindness that allows for natural, dynamic change to take place.

"Kindness" from this perspective, is a superb elixir that nourishes our discontinuities back to their natural wholeness. This takes amazing courage and tenacity. It is not an easy path, but perhaps the most real.

But there comes a time in both the healer's life and in the life of our path that we must begin to understand the role of *difference* in our lives.

It seems like this would be a small thing to understand and act upon: *This person is different from the way I am. They are totally valid in their current state.*

But in actuality, the very thought of this sets great forces within ourselves in motion, forces that do not want *difference* to continue.

To understand this, we have to make a connection between *difference* and *negativity* in the special way I am using it here. Let's begin by trying on a new understanding of the concept of *difference:* "difference" is not only the easy and apparent way we differentiate one thing from another, one subject from another object. It also—when *not* allowed to exist—erases the fundamental quality of uniqueness that is the bedrock expression of individuality in its highest sense: the true self.

In other words, the destruction of difference destroys the self and the self's connection to the all. When we cannot bear to let difference exist, the loss of "difference" is the loss of healing power itself.

Why should this be true? Why would we override difference so cavalierly if it is so important? When we say mentally to ourselves *What is wrong with this client?* we are jumping over, negating and destroying difference. Why do we do this? Why is it so difficult for us to simply sit back and say *I wonder who is in front of me, exactly as they are?*

We do it for two reasons: First, it is an attempt—unconscious though it may be—to separate ourselves from the client in order to reduce our own suffering. We reduce our suffering because we do not want to see the client's negative creation: it reminds us of our own suffering, those parts we are conscious of and those parts we are unconscious of, and we want to keep those areas hidden for what we believe is our own safety. Secondly, and equally, we don't want to have a relationship—and intimate relationship—with negativity at all! The rightful place of negative creation in the universe is something too threatening to consider. It is interesting to note that the Magi Process[6] actually *starts* with this understanding that negativity has a place in creation. Even though we work to change and modify it, we do this not to erase it as an illusion or mistake, *but because it is our choice!*

When we do this, when we invalidate the rightful place negativity has in creation, everything that follows, from the final diagnosis to the way in which we encounter the Tree of Life, is pathologized as well.

---

[6] The MAGI Process (The MAGI Process: A Nondual Method for Personal Awakening and the Resolution of Conflict, Shulman, The Foundation for Nonduality, 2016) is a thirty-eight-step, spiritually-dynamic methodology for the resolution of conflict and awakening. It is a way of participating in the creative machinery of the world. Since, from a nondual perspective, we are part of the world, made by the world and simultaneously making the world, to do the Process is to engage fully with reality. It is to drop into the programming language that made and makes the world as we know it. The thirty-eight steps of the MAGI Process are the actual answers about what is really here and who we are. They describe the essence of what you will find at every step of the journey when personal desires and questions come into contact with the great, impersonal vastness of reality. The first step, mentioned in the text above, acknowledges the fact that any change will be resisted by reality's built-in, non-personal inertia. Thus, the beginning of all enterprises of change must take this truth as its starting point and the foundation of the manifest world. It is important to understand that this inertia is not a negative or positive thing. It simply is.

Healing power occurs because of the unity of oneness and difference. Healing occurs in our tradition, from the creative moment of holding opposites, of allowing things to exist in such a way that they naturally change. The diagnostic process is a form of relationship that fosters both side of this seminal and *a priori* condition.

To hold both the validity of negativity's existence *and* the desire to change it, can only be done by coming to the point of being strong enough to approach the fire, as it were, to pick up the cup of poison and smell it, dip a finger into it, to see how it works, why it works, and if it needs to be feared forever. I am speaking metaphorically of course!

Creation/manifestation is always in the form of duality—either/or, left/right, good/bad and so on—so-called negative or shadow creation is always happening. The dark matter of the universe is such a condition.

If we are going to follow the path of intimacy, at some point—this is not for everyone at the same time!—we must begin to find a place for the negative in our lives. When we do not, and when that "do not" becomes repeated and programmatic, we must ask ourselves *why*.

When we find within ourselves the capacity to see that negative creation has a valid existence, when we encounter it in our clients or friends or ourselves, we see the whole person, the wise one and the neurotic one. We begin to see the power of *seeing* the negative, which is even more powerful than changing it in some ways. And we can only *see it* when we do not approach it with the immediate, instantaneous, unconscious desire to change it because we are afraid of it. There is great wisdom in seeing things as they are and the beginning of true change happens only when we see things as they are, which means seeing the actual existence of the negative, the *difference* in whatever form it may appear.

Negative creation is included in the pulsation of life. Life's nature is to pulsate, to be ambiguous, waving, curvilinear, alive. When we can do this, both our and the client's humanity, as expressed in the quality of *difference,* is allowed to exist. *Difference* is the nature of our true self and it is the foundation from which true healing flows. We stop creating from our own image of things. We stop healing from our own image of things.

Then, and only then, can the miracles that are a fundamental part of life, the miracles that *are* life itself, begin to exist and make a difference.

BEYOND THE NOW:
THE SECRET OF TIME

For many people—myself once included—there is a sense of purity associated with the concept of the now as a special point of time. The now is associated with a kind of innocence and spontaneity, a kind of instinctive, non-intellectual approach to each moment. This view of the now is often confused with what enlightenment or the awakened state is like.

Using a landmark—such as the concept of now or certain types of behaviors—is a way we have of trying to bring things into perspective, especially things that seem mysterious and ungraspable like enlightenment or being in the presence of god. By thinking in this way, we are trying to figure out what enlightenment is, to scale it down to size and domesticate it by some sort of insight or behavior in order to create a straight path to achieving what we want. We want a kind of feedback to tell us whether we are making progress toward our goal of liberation and if we can "get into the now," we believe we might just have a chance. Time permeates our ideas about what is and what is not enlightenment. There are schools of sudden and gradual enlightenment; secret studies one can or cannot do in deistic paths until the "time is right." There are times for ritual and ceremony that are based on the cycle of time, there are entire sutras in Tibetan Buddhism such as the *Kalacakratantra* or "The Wheel of Time," written about, among other things, time and the human condition. Time is our constant companion. It heralds beginnings and endings and so is in the center of human life.

We might begin to understand time and its role in our liberation if we can understand the difference between the type of time found in *satori*, which is a kind of peak experience of realization, and the time found in *enlightenment*, which is not an experience at all and includes walking in all sorts of geography, both physical, metaphysical and metaphorical.

Satori time is time in a state of shock. In satori, there is a sudden opening, an experience of everything falling apart or falling into place. Time seems to stop or not exist. It is a timeless moment. In deistic paths, there is a form of satori we could call "meeting God," or "falling to one's knees." It is what happened to Paul on the road to Damascus, to St Theresa of Avila. Meister Eckhart speaks of this too.

This vast opening to reality is extremely important on the path of spiritual growth. It offers not only a kind of deep insight, intuitive and spacious, but a relationship with what is, a kind of spiritual Eros that in one fell swoop makes all of our suffering and hard work worth it. It is the view from the mountain, from where you can see all of the territory in front of you. It is humbling and exhilarating. And by its very nature, it can also be addictive and limiting as well. This is because we believe—at that moment of considerable insight and Eros—to have seen a view of *all* of reality. But satori is really a deep view of one *feature* of reality. There is more; there is enlightenment.

The beginner especially makes this mistake easily, confusing deep, seemingly timeless insight with a deeply lived life *within* time. Enlightenment is more about walking the territory satori has shown you rather than simply looking at the colorful map it portrays from a particular position on the mountaintop.

Part of the reason for the difference between satori and enlightenment is the difference in the *who-is* in each of these circumstances. We can say that the *who-is* is the shape or form that the self-reflective part of our nature takes at any given moment, what it supposes its function is, and how dense its sense of reality and solidity is. In the primary experience of satori (since there are many types of satori), the mind of the practitioner is acutely aware of the *absence* of the central watcher, the always watchful ego-personality. We can simply understand this as an "opening to the big view," and whether this is a so-called nondual or deistic experience, the immense relief in discovering that the ego is simply a feature of total consciousness and not its true center, brings with it a profound sense of release. This is important and real. God is the center. The real is the center. The ego-personality, after having carried the load for so long, can sit back for once and take in the view, which is vast and touching. Satori is an experience to write home about or bring back vacation photos of. In comparison, enlightenment is somewhat boring and cannot be shared in this way.

Satori is attached to a *version* of the now, which we might call the "eternal now." In fact, we could say that it is the ego's discovery of this now that frames the experience we call satori. The personality suddenly discovers that it is not bound in chains from the past and can let go of the future. It is free to express its heart. As broad as satori is, however, it still needs conditions to be right, for particular features of reality to be highlighted or expressed. As it is still attached to conditions, it is still actually attached to time in a particular and limited way.

In other words, satori is still *conditional.* Satori-time is time still stuck in a preferred vision of time, which posits an "eternity" or timeless condition. So-called "eternal time" still has an opposite, however, called "linear time." It is this underpinning, the silent partner of timeless-time that satori-time is secretly attached to—if only by the sheerest of wisps of unuttered and even un-thought conceptualizations—an a-temporal condition that is "beyond time;" in other words, eternal, lasting and permanent.

Enlightenment-time is bound by time as well, and thus is well-acquainted with the passing of time in such ways as aging and death. Enlightenment-time is poignant, touching, intimate and alive in a way that satori-time, concerned with a sense of the eternal, is not. Satori-time, when it is preferred or attached to, is still concerned with a form of spiritual escape from linear time.

The "eternity" of enlightenment-time is the unredeemable past and the unknowable future…and the present moment that contains them both. This is the "big now," attached to nothing and un-save-able…and attached to everything and saved by everything. Enlightenment-time, in other words, accepts both the experience of the timeless moment and time as a form of, and commitment to, radical impermanence, constant birth and death as the basis of reality. Its heaven is not eternal but here and now in the human realm; its only dependable continuity, the constant presence—beyond all permanent sense of self—of radical impermanence and the gifts it brings.

Enlightenment-time sees no difference in all the temperatures of time: *past, present* or *future*. Memory is not enlightenment's enemy. Thinking about the future is not the enemy. There is no longer any enemy, only an infinite number of occasions in which to relate to what is.

In satori, thinking stops, or at least there seems to be a sort of silent core in the middle of the mind that thinks. In enlightenment, thinking continues, but the thinker is no longer so attached to the thoughts. The thinker is no longer entranced by the constantly present yet hardly seen, semi-consciousness "thought-container" that holds all of his or her thoughts, the ever-flowing *substratum* of thought: *These thoughts are mine.* It is not that the thinker doesn't claim ownership, but that thinking now leads toward less ownership rather than more because even the sense of ownership of thoughts is not a problem or a truism, but simply another part of the landscape as well.

It is the very absence of the habitual relationship with the *who-is* that makes satori an *experience*. The ego, formally so central that it seemed like the only possible view, is now off to the side or invisible. Yet, there is some sort of watcher of all of this who is delighted, in a spiritual sort of way. It is novel and fresh. Again, the freedom from time is based here on the novelty and freshness of time in its new incarnation.

While the voltage of the experience is still high, there is little thinking or conceptualizing that goes on about the experience. But once time passes, and the experience, like all experiences, lessens, thinking and conceptualizing return and the *who-is* now sets about trying to recapture the experience. The *who-is* changes from an enjoyer of no-time and the preciousness of passing time, to a *who-is* who worries, a *who-is* who is a detective who searches for what now is *time past.*

In a sense, conceptualized and remembered satori has no relationship with the changing scene. It *thinks* it does, since it now views itself as open in some way, but subtly and sometimes not so subtly, it rejects views, feelings, and thoughts that don't fit in with its initial, penetrating and powerful experience. It rejects the spiritual gravity that seeks to pull satori downward, resisting in a sense, the natural consequence of living in the passing of time.

Enlightenment, on the other hand, is willing to have a relationship with this changing world. Enlightenment is an old hand, someone who's been through the movie many times, and so difficulties such as aggressive attachment to an experience, are not rejected out of hand. It is workable to meet the enemy, to have tea with Satan and sympathy for the devil. From an enlightened perspective, we even understand the attraction the ego has for this state of awareness. We see that the ego is expressing a limited—but potent—form of love, spoken in the language of separateness. We see it when it is there and are not afraid of it. There is nothing this experience of the loss of separateness or of union could spoil, since there is no territory to defend. We are thrown or not thrown by it. Both are OK.

Satori shakes things up; without it, the bread might not get leavened. But what we are after is not the leavening, but the bread itself. The bread does not exist in the eternal: that is what makes it so delicious! Yet, by including even satori-time in its vast view, the enlightened view brings even more to this nourishing feast.

As this process goes on, we begin to see time differently. Time in satori is dramatic. Time in enlightenment passes. I don't mean to make this sound dull. Its passing is bitter and sweet, enormously comforting and a bit sad as well. Life and death are a bit sad, but ultimately very alive. It is important to understand that there *is* only present time. Any other view is a form of fantasy. All of our thoughts, whether about the past or the future, are happening in this very moment. There is no effort needed to find the now: It is the only place in time we actually inhabit. We see this "big-tent now," this holistic now, when every passing thing is included in our view. Our thoughts about the past are happening now. Our thoughts about the future are happening now. It is when we don't know this fully and firmly, that we live in the reverie that the past is present. This is a form of neurosis that psychotherapy—which might be called an exquisite healing into the now—helps so much with. This has deep implications for how we heal, for the actual process of healing and how it takes place. As we experience "satori brought down to earth," the quotidian, the perfectly imperfect, we enter the world of real being, of feeling the divine all around us.

Although we all think of enlightenment and surrendering to God as very difficult, esoteric and perhaps distant, there is something in all human beings that is drawn to this vision of reality since it is at the core of reality. It is how we are actually organized as beings. As we see how the timeless moment and moment-in-time rise together inseparably, as we hold it all, our purpose becomes apparent, our human heart can speak.

The secret of time is that it can be bent by the human heart. This is not a perceptual matter, but a way of saying that as different organs and senses perceive different frequencies and vibrations, so the human heart is the organ that can pierce the meniscus of ordinary, simple-stepped time to show us what time looks like and how it flows when the heart is free of conceptions. It lets us know that we are approaching wholeness not because it is a personal feeling, but because the heart is the organ—or metaphor—that leads us from the personal to the transcendent-personal. Satori-time still exists, but as a feature of the wholeness of time. So, we do not live in the fantasy that time doesn't pass, or that time doesn't matter, but—just as the notes on a page of music are not the music—so satori-time is only a feature of the universe and not the simultaneous play of the universe itself.

In an *awakening* or *realizing* state, the living quality of time becomes apparent. We see that our very being is time, that time and objects, and time and thoughts, and time and feelings are all one thing. These things are not happening *in* time but *are* time. You might say that we give up ideas of eternity for the constant and touching actual passage of time and give up the passage of time—seeing its wholeness and simultaneity—to participate in the great dance that goes on forever. The heart holds our attitude toward openness and closed-ness and is the organ-metaphor that lets us encompass every changing state and thereby lets us see, feel and participate in the whole of our being and therefore, in the whole of reality.

Satori, enlightenment, awakening, surrender to God, self-realization are all words to describe the basic movement of opening of the spiritual heart. Time changes in each of these states. Satori, which at first can seem like true open-heartedness, broadens in enlightenment to open-heartedness in which all flavors of opening, from fully opened to fully closed, are included in its broad reach. It no longer relies on conditions but is essentially condition-less or even condition-full.

It is as if you are looking at the stars in a black night sky, sending out their rays, blue, slightly red, a bit green or yellow. And you think, using your three-dimensional mind, the limited *who-is*, how the light emitted far in the past has traveled light years to reach your eyes. Then, with your heart widened by the beauty of the scene, since that is what beauty is for, to open the heart, you start seeing in four, five, six, perhaps ten dimensions. Time falls apart and you glimpse eternity, and you see suddenly that what looks like cause and effect separated by moments of time is not really that way, but simultaneously exposed faces, facets of a single gem. Everything is happening at once. Then you realize these stars have their end in their beginning and seeing further, you see new beginnings in their endings. Soon endings and beginnings lose their meaning as all the gates open at once and time loses its meaning; now, birth and death, first star glow and heat death all appear in the sky at once. The black night is filled with light, more light than you can ever have imagined and, overwhelmed, you see the truth. Then, because satori-time is not enough, does not have the human touch, you walk back into the house, and your eyes, getting used to the light in the kitchen again, see a member of your family. They are not the universe: they are themselves. They will live and die and you with them. Is eternity more precious than this? And yet, once you allow yourself to feel that preciousness, eternity comes knocking on the door again. You open the door and a star is there. Stars on the outside, stars on the inside. The constant universal and particular dance, the arising of the world, over and over again.

IT IS I, MYSELF, THAT ILLUMINATES THE ABSOLUTE... AND IT IS THE ABSOLUTE THAT GIVES ME THIS LIGHT

I and the absolute

Ram Dass tells a story—if I remember it correctly—about visiting his brother, who happened to be in a mental institution at the time. His brother told Ram Dass that he, the brother, was Christ. Ram Dass had no problem with this. The only problem, he told his brother, was that he thought he was the only one.

In the on-going exploration of reality through meditation, I came upon the thought that makes up the title of this essay: *It is I, myself, that illuminates the absolute and it is the absolute that gives me this light.* I was even nervous *thinking* this thought. It seemed so egocentric. Even so, I decided to go on, since my commitment is to follow reality wherever it leads me.

My experience of living with this thought, however, was very different from what I thought it might be. First, we notice that the statement is circular: no one "owns" this light. It is instead, a point of view, in fact, a point of view from the personal perspective.

Prior to this thought, I felt deeply peaceful looking at the manifest world from the perspective of the absolute, that is, the manifest world as the simultaneous upwelling of the absolute's absolutely unalterable and singular fate: to become many.

From this perspective, the manifest world was an expression of total creativity: some of it sublime, some of it terrible, but all of it perfect in its imperfection. This view left me free to accept everything that I saw while simultaneously, engaging in the morality that was embedded in the non-thinking absolute, which is to say, a morality that did not come from any secondhand source but one that was more like a stone or a river: an undeniable feature of reality. So, I could speak out, I could accept or reject, I could take any form or function of which I was capable, but mainly, I could melt my neurotic tendency to judge, to create hierarchies. I could love.

When this sentence came upon me, I had the new experience of *looking at the absolute* from the perspective of this self-same personal state—not the tortured or anguished personal, but from what I have called in the past, the "personal with no history," which is the rectified personal self. By "rectified" I do not mean it was perfect or without imperfections. On the contrary, the *entire* personal self was present in this looking, but by being its total self, the totality of its being, this version of the personal self was self-illuminated, a fancy way of saying that it was stable, a feature of the world, unique and not-unique at the same time, honored, held, appreciated and loved.

When I looked back at the absolute from this position, the absolute seemed utterly dark to me. Darkness does not even begin to suggest the utter lack of light I perceived in this place—or I should say *non-place*. Every landmark was gone. It was utterly without boundedness. It was—to simply metaphorize it a bit—a river of blackness, of lifeblood, of a force that traveled through everything, every manifest, physical thing, and was intimately tied to the urge to be itself. It was the force that united beings in sex, that produced generations, that was the furrow of crops and fertility. It was, as the Dao de Ching mentions, the "valley spirit of the feminine," inexhaustible.

Of course, this was not "feminine" in any sense except in the limited words we have in this dualistic world. It was dark. It was unmoving yet ever flowing. It was beyond positive and negative, beyond yes or no. It did not surrender to any category and could not be corralled for any purpose except its own.

By seeing this, the personal self was transformed as well. It became silent. It was holding hands with the unexplainable, unknowable. It became filled with the mud of the delta, the billions of curlicues that hold each other in the web of being. And there was no web, no being. But the personal self was dignified by it, stood up straighter, was neither in the personal or transcendent world, was like a tree in a field no one visits, looking out over the extension of its roots, no matter how far away.

Ram Dass' brother had half the story and having only that half, a kind of craziness inhabited him. The "myself" in the title sentence is, of course, this creation that springs from the absolute itself as the creation it is powerless to avoid. It is the self that sees the great continuity of reality and therefore is not personally owned. A personal self that belongs to the absolute, an absolute—contrary to its gigantic name—that owes its existence to my eyes, my ears, my heart and my sex, a continuity I did not own, and which did not own me. What a situation! It was as if I found myself in the Great Seed of All Being, dark, underground, muddy and, in every way, nothing I could "attain" or keep to myself. And within that nothingness, I had two legs, a belly and back, preferences and joys and hands I kept muddy

with my own endless acts of creation, just like the dark place
I came from.

Doing

The language of spiritual questing has long been
infiltrated by the idea of "surrender." Though "effort" is
often invoked, it is seen mainly as a pathway to surrender
and its ultimate companion, *just being*. "Just sitting"
(*shikantaza*), the Muslim idea of giving over to Allah's Will,
the Christian and Jewish ideas of "doing God's work" and
others, all look at this state of *being* as a kind of ultimate—
"*doing*" being relegated, at least in the spiritual hierarchy, as
something "less than." *Being* seems closer to the divine. But
we can posit a new idea: that everything in the manifest
world is actually *doing*, that existence itself is *doing*, but this
doing is doing-without-a-goal.

When we view *doing* from this perspective, the view
that *everything in the manifest world is pure doing*, it surprisingly
does not accrue to the personal ego so much as to the self-
nature of everything in the manifest world. This is how
everything wears or expresses its "original face," which is
identical to its original function. This is creativity for its own
sake and, since every manifest thing is righteously efforting
to express its self-nature beyond the layers thrust upon it by

other external agencies, each thing can become aware that it is part of the web of being, the inter-relatedness or *continuity/density* of all things. The phrase "continuity/density" is the ground idea of the seamless interconnectedness of all things (continuity) and the simultaneous, inevitable and co-arising feature of this continuity, namely, individuals and individual things and lives.

Further, this *doing-without-a goal*, this pure agency of manifestation and expression, means that all things have a "center" or sense of self that is the inseparable companion to the *continuity;* these identities, whether person, rock, stream or tree, exist more by their interactions and relationships with the *continuity* as a whole, than as actual, independent manifestations of stand-alone beings. The child's development from dependent to self-organization is connected in every way to his or her relationship with their environment: parents, culture, education, moment in time and the extended family of every object in the world. Without this *continuity* there is no self. It is as if there is a sort of social unconsciousness that we only awaken from as we are in relationship.

So, from this point of view, *each-thing-doing,* is a non-egoic event in that it is a feature of the *continuity,* in union with it. This type of egoic event drinks the fluid of the darkness of the absolute to both create and fill the many nodes or *densities* that make up the whole, the flowing quality that is the substance of all creativity and the origin of its original impulse. This doing is without strain. It is energetic and alive. It gazes back toward this dark river as its mother, as that horizon toward which it moves. *Being and beyond being* guides the actions of the manifest world. We *do,* in order to emulate and unite with the unattainable and unlocatable. It was why we were born.

Nothing "just be-s." Being and doing are united when every manifest thing *doing* and the dark river are united. It is the dynamic still-point when everything in the frame is moving at the exact same speed. It is what makes the world work. This is why we revolve around the small center of our own lives on a planet that revolves around our sun in a galaxy that revolves around an empty center in the constellation Vega, an empty or dark attractor that is the center of our pinwheel life. We could—paradoxically—say that we only achieve *being* when we *do* without a goal, when we see it is our nature to *do.*

From birth to death, our lives are filled with this *doing* and with or without our personal consciousness, the continual stream of *doing* within this *continuity,* we go on being as expressions of all that is.

FACTS AND SIGNS
IN A MEANINGLESS WORLD

A meaningless universe is a terrifying thing to a human being and the search for meaning is meant to give shape and stature to human life, to protect it, in a sense, from the depressing regularity of the arbitrariness of life: Good people die while dictators and devils live on; accidents take precious lives; disease takes some and lets others live. Machines fail, people fall from the sky. The tornado whips by. The hurricane arrives. The earthquake begins.

Probably every person who has ever embarked on a spiritual journey has done so because they were compelled to find meaning in their life. In my own case, anxiety attacks—moments of panic and confusion—caused me to seek psychotherapeutic help: I wanted to understand how my mind worked and what was at the bottom of these attacks. Add to that the fact that knowledge of the world and the self fascinated me from childhood onward, and I was ripe for the spiritual quest to begin.

Once it begins, the search for meaning establishes the territory. The journey of inquiry will travel between the poles of meaning and its often-unwelcome brother, meaninglessness. In other words, a quest for meaning has a foreground—in this case "meaning"—and a background— "meaninglessness." In this way, the entire universe is constrained, unconsciously, between these two opposites and the success of the journey is determined by how close one comes to the preferred pole of *meaning*. The shape and direction of the journey in a sense becomes pre-determined, and through this lens, all events that do not lead to *meaning* as the final goal appear chaotic, meaningless, without rhyme or reason. As a friend of mine is fond of saying "You get the answer your questions ask for." The search for *meaning* always seeks to find meaning and reject meaninglessness.

However, the search for *meaning* creates its own difficulties. Because the arbitrariness of the universe is so unnerving, so mysterious, so without structure, we seek with all our might to hold chaos at bay. Thus, we become attached to meaning, the preferred pole of the gradient between meaning and meaninglessness. We are causally confused. How and why do things happen? Who is in charge? God? If so, where is God and how do we communicate with God? Gods? Buddha? Nature? Physics?

So, part of our hoped-for passage into *meaning* requires that we read into nature to find the gods, into texts to reveal the secret message, into events to tease out the threads of karma, all in an effort to throw our lives up upon a screen on which we can plot out our existence and say, "this happened for a reason."

Meaning as an organizing principle has had many successes of course. Our technological and scientific achievements, which can cause disasters both physical and spiritual, have also saved many people from illness and disaster. And it is true that the search for *meaning* has an important function in the spiritual quest. But ultimately, the *meaning/meaningless* axis limits the universe from showing us what it truly is and who we truly are.

When we separate *meaning* from *meaninglessness,* we unconsciously intensify our longing, desperation and confusion. We begin to believe that what we desperately want—*meaning*, the divine, surrender, peace—is far away and secreted within the myriad paths of the world. We must therefore find "the one true path," or the "one true text," or the "one true teacher." The world in this way is reduced to a collection of puzzle pieces we are required to put together if we are to find the nourishment our hearts, minds, and bodies truly need and desire.

The tricky thing here is that this search for meaning is an important thing. In my own case, for example, this passionate search focused me. It showed me the benefits of discipline. It brought me to several communities of seekers and teachers who leant support and sustenance. But when all is said and done, what I have understood is that meaning, in its opposition to meaninglessness, is not the end result or end vision of the spiritual search for wholeness. "Wholeness," in other words, is something different from "meaning." We might even say that meaning and meaningless must come together for there to be wholeness. While the search for *meaning* teaches us how to think and discriminate and begins the task of teaching us right from wrong and how to think about the world in a positive way, it is ultimately an obstacle.

This good thing—*meaning*—like many other good things, when in excess, becomes a powerful constriction upon our lives. While *meaning* makes the personal self larger or more expanded as personal consciousness penetrates what it considers the "unknown," it also separates us from true wholeness. At its worst, the exclusive search for *meaning* can make us crazy beings, insane converts to the religion of comparison, of the second-hand, of "my way or the highway." It narrows the world down from a living and changing thing to a diorama. It halts the world instead of making it possible to find freedom within it. It tends, in its quest to understand, to tear the world into ever smaller and smaller pieces, to try to find God's (or reality's) design in every smaller and smaller detail in order to finally get it right so that we are allowed into heaven or some awakening state, as if these states were a locked room and we, the beggars at the door. The whole point of heaven is that it is an open room. In fact, only from the belief that the continuum of *meaning/meaninglessness* describes something real, does it appear to be a room at all, with an "inside" or "outside," and that we are waiting to be let in—when our actions are approved, our dance steps are "correct," and we have found "meaning."

Let us, instead, begin to think about it in this way: meaning is a special kind of pleasure, which we are free to choose. But it has nothing to do with "the truth" in any absolute way. Instead, meaning is a way to organize the world, a world which, from the awakening position, is already exquisitely organized.

The search for meaning is a developmentally correct occupation for every being. From certain parts of our personality and at certain chronological ages, this search is of vital importance. And within that search are the pleasures of longing, of finding and losing, of discovery and desire, of unraveling a mystery. The problem begins when we confuse finding meaning with finding the truth, and what we believe "the truth" we find will save us from.

Because this view of the "search for the truth," when it is confused with the "search for meaning," is so all-encompassing in its believability, it subtly colors all of our perceptions and experience. We begin adventures and projects, have insights and go on quests always in order to find the smallest unit, building block, or essential component or, contra-wise, to see the biggest vista. We want "The Truth," "The Meaning," with capital letters, so that life, with its dangers, suffering and pitfalls, becomes a safer, more manageable thing. So, we begin to look at the world and all that is contained in it, the facts of the world, as it were, as the particles and particulars of this faith. We become connoisseurs not of facts, but of what we think facts represent: the secret of the passage to truth. We become connoisseurs of signs.

From an awakening point of view, however, the paradigm changes: Facts are not signs signifying something else, some secret meaning or an arrow pointing to some profundity. Instead, all signs are facts. The world is not a guidebook to its meaning: the world's meaning is in its existence. In fact, "meaning" on this level is equal to "meaninglessness" as simply another facet of an infinite world. They are both features of the world.

So, if this quest along the continuum of *meaning/ meaninglessness* is not the final or even best way to find and lead an authentic and good life, an enlightened life, what is?

Let me see if I can give you an idea. The tree has no meaning. Instead, it has something much greater: it is an expression of the entire universe, in this moment, right now. On every level, it is connected to what makes the universe the universe, and us us. Within, its molecules get transported from here to there. Hunger is present and satiety is accomplished. Insects are protected by it, fed by it. Birds have their babies within it. Squirrels, too. Chipmunks that congregate around its base, picking up seeds, are spied there by raptors. The tree is a supermarket for the hawk.

All the great themes of manifest existence are present as the tree is simply and magnificently itself: growth, from seed to decay, light and dark within sunlight and shade. Thirst. Shape, form, function, perfection suited to its environment. And more important than all of these, this tree is the expression of a mysterious desire, the mysterious desire of life to live, of existence to exist. It lives and wants to live, yet it dies. It is tragic in a way, as beautifully spoken in the language of a tree's existence as any Shakespearean play. The more we look—and the more we love what we see—the less "meaning" we find and the more inter-relationship we see and are satisfied by. Instead of the tree "meaning something," we find that it means everything.

One of the differences between the search for meaning and the recognition of inter-relationship is that in the search for meaning we are always separate to some degree; the poignancy of the search actually requires, to some extent, that we always remain somewhat separate from our final goal. In other words, the seeker seeks. Although hoped for, the seeker and the sought-for rarely become united. In true inter-relationship, not hindered by the preconception of *meaning*, each thing is purely itself, and the true relationship between things is built on this separateness that is actually the *foundation* of relationship.

But outside of that paradigm, beyond the circumscribed circle of limitation proposed by the intersection of meaning and meaninglessness, the world is already one thing, and the deepest pleasure comes from the unending discovery of our complete unity with the manifest world.

The world is God. The world is enlightenment. We don't discover these things *within* the world, as if the truth had burrowed into the earth and we had to dig it out. Instead, the world in the process of its wholeness is the wholeness itself. It refuses—in its openness—to be labeled as "this" or "that." It moves onward because onward is its meaning. It stops because stopping is its pleasure and its meaning. It lives and dies because these things are its nature. To discover our own nature and the nature of the world we must see what is in front of our eyes.

So how do we make this transition from the axis of meaning/meaninglessness to an awakened perspective which includes the pleasure of meaning but is not limited by it?

One of the secrets, I believe, is in looking at our preferences. When we do that, we enter the dynamic stream of life. In this case, our preference is for meaning as opposed to meaninglessness. It is inescapable: when the world is split into "this" and "that," there is always a preference. And from this preference the wholeness of the world is destroyed. In the case we are speaking about we prefer *meaning alone*, with all its limitations and small views, of course. The remedy, then, is to explore *meaninglessness*, the great monster we believe we must destroy in order to live, well, a life that has meaning.

Years ago, I did an experiment: Typically, whenever anyone asked me for the time, I'd simply look at my watch and tell them. But I realized that in the moment before I looked, I did not know the time. So, I allowed myself to fall deeply into this not-knowing to see what it felt like.

"What time is it?" someone would ask.

"I don't know," I'd say.

The more I did this, the more I reveled in not-knowing and let this delight spread out to the rest of my life.

"What is the meaning of life?"

"I don't know..."

"When will you die?"

"I don't know..."

"Is there a God?"

"I don't know!"

Strangely enough, the more I sank into not-knowing, the more whole, the more free, the more integral I became. In fact, I became more intelligent: when I needed to know, I knew. When I didn't, I simply didn't. No fear, no search for meaning. Something new began to form in me then, something I am still learning to let grow within me, the world growing all around me.

Now *not-knowing* and *meaninglessness* are somewhat different: *not-knowing* is somewhat cool to the hot and reducing fire that is *meaninglessness*. *Meaninglessness,* which can be likened to a boundary-less state, when conjoined with *meaning,* which has a feeling of *continuity,* because there is a "there" there, is the true wholeness of the world. Not nihilistic, not depressed, but dynamically alive to joy, to grief, to life and death.

When not jailed by the search for meaning exclusively, the me who is that tree I spoke about appears in the world. The me who is *not* that tree, who walks and talks and loves and hates, appears as well. Oneness and separateness. Boundless and Bounded. Together and apart. And a deep moral sense, not learned from a book, but from my heart, appears to guide me as well.

Now, as I finish writing this on a cold Cape Cod morning, I see sunlight appearing through the clouds, falling on my front street. This will make my wife happy: She loves the light.

DESIRE

People often think that though the spiritual journey begins in desire it should end in desirelessness. From this perspective, certain types of desires and passions, such as the passion for God, for awakening and enlightenment, for self-realization and surrender, are good, especially at the beginning of the quest. But *desire* in general seems to be a soldier in the enemy's troop, if not the Supreme Commander of the opposition. In this view, these other desires, for things like power, sex, food, and even for realization itself, are emotions and needs that will keep the doors of liberation firmly shut. But this is a misunderstanding of both desire and desirelessness and its function throughout the spiritual journey.

We might say that we are made of desire and always will be made of desire. In fact, from my point of view, desire as an impulse, the impulse to move forward, to survive, to stay alive, never changes. What changes is the *who-is* that owns this desire.

Many people make the mistake of thinking that their *who-is*, the person they are now, is the same one who moves throughout the years of the spiritual path, that somehow something we call "I" or "myself" moves through this journey like a train on a track: The track doesn't change, nor does the train. Instead, we continue traveling and eventually wind up someplace else.

But this image is incorrect. If we were to keep the image of the train and the track, more accurately we'd have to say that to get to where we are going, sometimes the track disappears, sometimes the train disappears. Sometimes you turn into a leopard or a crocodile or mouse. Sometimes you are required to get off the train and look around, sometimes to cry and other times to laugh.

The self is changed by the journey to find the self. The self that starts the journey is not the one who ends the journey, if an ending can even be talked about. The journey is designed to change you into the one who can walk into the holy of holies, who finds the real self because they *are* the real self, whose Buddha-nature is evident because that is the only thing that is there; who is fully human because they have *become* human, through great toil, courage, humility and laughter.

But through all of this, desire remains because desire is the bones of life.

Baruch Spinoza, the Dutch philosopher, used the *conatus* to describe this important aspect of reality. Here is the definition of this word from Wikipedia:

Conatus is Latin for effort; endeavor; impulse; inclination; tendency; undertaking or striving. It is a term used in early philosophies of psychology and metaphysics to refer to an innate inclination of a thing to continue to exist and enhance itself. This "thing" may be mind, matter or even a combination of both.

Conatus is desire, the desire to continue and endure, and it is the fundamental quality all created things have in common, whether they are bird, beast, human, vegetable or mineral. The material world—ourselves and our psychology included—resists change. We resist it because we all know in our deepest hearts that change into non-existence is inevitable. The evidence of the disappearance of the material world is all around us.

This *desire* that is at the heart of all things—to conserve the structure and information they are (for example, our structure is our body; our information is our notion of who we are)—is not personal to us. That is, the force of desire does not belong to us anymore than the air we breathe belongs to us. We make use of the air. You could say that we are an instrument for using air or for air using us. In the same way, we make use of desire and desire makes use of us. Of course, as our *who-is* changes, we have different relationships to the same quality of desire.

As young children we might have desired cotton candy. I know I did. And we felt that if we did not get it, we would: 1) die, 2) be unhappy for the rest of our lives, or 3) forever hate the person who refused us this treat. We believed this because our sense of self was exactly the same size, as it were, as these perceptions. Now, looking back at those same reactions from an adult point of view, we have so much more freedom. The size of our sense of self is much larger than that refusal and we have room within our psyche-soma to hold this unfulfilled desire without breaking as we did when we were a child.

Our *who-is* changed. And during the spiritual journey, the world does not change so much as our *who-is* changes, our capacity changes. But our *conatus* does not.

In the great wisdom books of Buddhism and in the tales of Hasidic masters, we find time and again beings who have exchanged one desire, a small one, for a larger desire. We start out wanting to be free for our own purposes. This is right and proper. We end up wanting freedom for all beings since more and more we identify with all beings. Bodhisattvas and great rabbis all derive pleasure from helping others. In fact, we could say that the desire for pleasure—another aspect of the *conatus*—not only remains, but strengthens, both in its resolve, focus and clarity. In Judaism, this is called *kavannah*, a word that might be translated as "devotional-intentionality." In Buddhism it is the basis for the bodhisattva's vow to save all sentient beings.

Before this understanding, desire and desirelessness might be confused as two mutually exclusive things. For example, we might see desirelessness as the capacity to be in the moment, allowing the moment to be as it is. Desire on the other hand, could be seen as the ever-increasing passion we have to be with God or to experience our total self, to belong, to be free. It might be equated with having the intensity and inner spirit to stand up for what we believe even in the face of opposition.

Yet, we cannot have one without the other. Desirelessness without desire is dead, pale, aloof, intellectual, conceptual. Desire without desirelessness is all gonads. Passion without thought. Action without consequence.

As the *who-is* changes, as we have more capacity, desire begins to look like desirelessness. But the difference is this: desirelessness is not the *absence* of desire, but the *openness* to the energy of *all* desires. We might say that desirelessness is the state of being transparent to all desires. We allow our desires to move consciously through us without being acted upon by any of them. This means that we are no longer ruled by all desires but, as living beings who are separate and can choose, choose those desires that fit in with the intelligence our *who-is* has grown to be. This is freedom.

The final point of this is to say that desirelessness and desire remain, an interlocked pair, throughout the spiritual journey. You cannot have one without the other. When our *who-is* is strictly personal, this pairing seems to be entirely derived from the world of personal preference. But when our *who-is* also has the awareness of the transcendent-impersonal, we find that the axis of desire-desirelessness is built into the fabric of the universe and is part of its full glory.

Desire is not the enemy. It is true that there are portions of the spiritual journey where desire must be carefully controlled. The important point to remember, however, is that the ultimate goal of the spiritual path is not to erase desire in some sort of dream of freedom. Real freedom, unlike its fantasy counterpart, consists of being all of who you are and more important, having the who-you-are be all of you, the total you. The human you.

CONSTANT PRAYER:
THE CONTINUAL MOMENT
OF SURRENDER

There are spiritual formulations, hidden questions or statements really, that are so powerful that we avoid contemplating them because our unhealed egos—ever watchful for anything that might upset the applecart—instinctively know that these questions might destroy the safe harbor we have found on the coast of our chosen path. These statements reveal often unthought beliefs that we carry with us no matter which approach to spirituality we choose, whether it is one in which we interact with God as a separate entity or being, which has surrender to a higher power as its goal, or one that professes nonduality and has personal enlightenment as its objective. Let's call these beliefs *Things That Should Not Be Spoken*.

Here is one from a deistic perspective:

God only exists when I pray.

Is this a blasphemous statement? It would seem so from the mindset of a deistic path that tends to relate to God as a formless, eternal, indivisible entity, separate from the perceiver. But what is revealed, if we consider this statement for more than a moment, is a hidden belief we may not have stated consciously to our self or others: Shouldn't the very essence of God, the thing that makes God *God,* be that God exists whether I am aware of God or not? Isn't God an objective entity? If God is somehow dependent upon *me,* then who is there to offer me safety and support in times of trouble? Who is there to greet my most vulnerable and suffering self? If God needs *me* or something I do in order to exist, then is God merely a projection of my subjective self? A fantasy that arises from my inner child self who is still looking for a perfect parent to nurture and accept the little being I still am? There are many people who believe this to be true and because of this, avoid the line of inquiry that leads to beliefs such as these.

In Buddhism—as an example of a nondual approach to spirituality—we encounter a similar, though often deeply hidden, belief that likewise can be revealed by entertaining a specific statement or formulation that is challenging to some part of our unhealed ego, namely, that there is a "place," a condition, a state called "enlightenment," and that our spiritual path is to *get there, to get to that place.* Even if we do not subscribe to this consciously, chances are there is some part of all of us that entertains that thought. We could say that part of this misconception about enlightenment is the belief—unstated, perhaps unthought or even consciously denied—that enlightenment *already* exists and that we move toward that omega point. It is not something invented by the meditator, but a stream of being-ness we slip into the way time slips into eternity. We are working toward and waiting for the "click" that turns everything around and announces that we too have arrived in the sacred land. The statement that might bring this hidden and dangerous problem (dangerous to our belief of course,) to the surface might be something like:

Enlightenment doesn't exist. There is no place or condition where enlightenment can be found. Our spiritual path doesn't lead away from ignorance: it leads toward it.

Talk about getting into trouble! And yet I say that God is reborn every time we pray and there is no enlightenment as long as there is enlightenment.

Unless we come to grips with these hidden beliefs and find a worthy tool to deal with these unstated stumbling blocks, we are in a dream of freedom and not freedom itself. In this dream of God, since the deistic path works with the condition of separateness and the seeming absence of God, finding God means that we have discovered that there *is* *someone there.* In the dream of enlightenment, which works on the simplest level with the problem of the existence of the ego and the separate self as a stumbling block, we find there is no one there. In this dream, we are finally free of our selfhood and now tangibly part of "the universe." In both cases, *we* is the important, operative term: *we* feel God; *we* overcome our ego and find awakening. Each is a way of looking at each path as a hoped-for end of suffering from different perspectives. But suffering can only really pale in the light of truth. And unless, sooner or later, we come to grips with the contradictions inherent in these statements, we cannot achieve either the surrender we long for or the bright perspective we hope we will find.

Certain roads are the best roads to get to certain places. In rain, we wear something waterproof and hold umbrellas. In winter, heavy coats. In spring and summer, less clothing. Our diet changes from roots to leaves as the weather gets warmer. Things change and being in life means that we change with these changes, we continue on, so to speak, not because we have no will or center of our own, but because being intimate with life, being *appropriately* alive, is our goal and our pleasure. This simple thing, the fact that we feel best when we are contiguous with life, coherent and in constant touch, is an expression of the fact that even as everything changes, everything remains connected in an ever-changing, flexible web of being, which keeps its unitive features even as it morphs from one shape to another. From this perspective, everything—every knot in the web, every stitch in reality's embroidery, is a possible portal to wholeness. From this point of view, every discipline or practice is a potential doorway, every detail of the physical world an expression of the divinity, the self-illuminated quality of the whole in every detail.

But what we all really need is exactly what our unhealed egos turn away from: we need to entertain these statements, actually embrace them as catalysts that can reduce our fear of life as it is and by doing that, present us with a direct road to illumination, whether we call that light "being with God," or "finding the true self."

Because life is a continuity and cannot be other than that, every bit of life invites us to freedom. Yet, we miss these doorways or even better, we miss recognizing that being exactly where we are, using total, radical honesty about where we are, *is the doorway itself.*

Instead, most of us are engaged in a different pursuit, a pursuit that brings along with it the misbegotten idea that we must *be a certain way* in order to enter the gate to heaven. Whether that means giving up the ego before we can pass on to nirvana, or being a totally blameless person, we do not truly trust who we are or that the universe did not make us defective or broken so that we could be something other than who we are but in order to *be who we are.*

Being who we are is entirely different than giving ourselves license to be any way we choose. Being who we are means we have awakened to who we are, that we have chosen to kindly and honestly be who we are, present our self as such because it is true and real and, in its own way, as whole as we can be in that moment in time. To help us do this, we need the proper tools, tools that can help us no matter what path we choose and especially a tool that works with the fact that who we are changes constantly both because we are part of life and life changes constantly and also because the self is actually not a steady, inviolable, concrete thing but—how should I put it?—a *suggestion*, a gestalt, a pattern made up of pieces that are not us but which join, moment by moment, to give us a sense of identity. We could say that this self-identity, changing moment by moment, is the perfect vehicle for the continuity of a constantly changing world. Prayer is the practice that stands in between the deistic paths and the nondual paths, bringing honesty and progress to each. It is one of the most excellent vehicles when done in the way I will describe it.

Each person who is on the path to awakening or surrender must, if they are going to achieve their goal, come to grips with the part of them that cleaves their very soul in two in order to fit in to some preconceived idea of what enlightenment is or how to relate authentically to the divinity. Prayer is useful because of the largeness and largess of its container: in other words, it is big enough to contain the truth.

To stand in prayer is to stand in the presence of who we are, just as we are, with our problems and aspirations, with our passionate desires and our fearful and frightened parts, with every "who" that we are along the spectrum of the possible. Whether we are applying to the Godhead for help with the alleviation of suffering or intoning a sutra to Buddha in order to inspire the best in our self, to the echo back of our own Buddha, only when we bring all of our self just as we are to the prayer itself, will the connections that need to be made, be made; only then will we recognize the *already-in-place* connections as they are or, to put it another way, recognize that God is already here. To be contiguous with life, which is to say, surrendered to God or self-illuminated, is to be honest. It is to invest in the moment as it is, whether that is a moment of loss or gain.

Again, from a spiritual perspective, this is true because the world is one continuity, and everything is important and holy when allowed to exist in the light of day, as it were. We don't need an ocean to be grateful for water: a glass of it will do. In the same way, when we see correctly, revealing just who we are to our own self, it is sufficient to open our eyes to the truth of our lives. It is not because doing a prayer in some special way brings us to some special place or lets us meet a special being, but because prayer, when done from the perspective I am suggesting, brings us to the display of life itself and life itself *is* a million, million ways of actually seeing God if that is your wish, or of standing in the Buddha dharma, if that is your way. This grand connection, omnipresent and available, brings to the foreground that which cannot be lost. More specifically, it unites the foreground of our separate self with this continuity of the background so that, each is vital to each other. The separate, personal self and the no-personal-self join hands to awaken us to the constant presence of light, whether that light is called *Ha-shem*, Allah, God, Buddha or whatever other holy name you can think of. Or even silence itself. And, equally important, it allows us to see that every created thing is a doorway to wholeness and that each path, despite the difference in name, practice and attitude, is really the universe's kind attention to us, serving us a meal that is especially prepared for our metabolism, for our sense of taste and our need for nutrition.

In fact, taking this particular thought one radical step further, we could say that one of the purposes of a human being is to bring warmth and aliveness to a universe that is completely willing, but which sits in deep disinterestedness, a kind of open nothingness. We are the ones who teach the world to bow and wrap up the immense power of life in a heart that opens every fist.

So, how do we do this? How do we pray so that we can draw closer to God or heal the unhealed sense of self so that the Buddha-land becomes *our* land? In actuality, the rules of this type of praying are rather simple, perhaps only two in number. First, we need to acknowledge that, held deeply in the continuity of life, we change and morph from one relationship with the separate self to another. Sometimes we are "condensed" in a way that highlights the differences between our self and the outside world; between our self and the divinity (or enlightened state as we believe it to be). So sometimes subject and object are prominent: We actually feel the separation between our self and the world and indeed, our self and the state of spiritual awareness we want to be in. Sometimes the separation between subject and object is much milder and not the most prominent decider of who we take ourselves to be. Sometimes we do not notice the sunset: it passes by, sun sinks, and another day is gone. Other times, that same sun, red and flattened as it sinks into a horizon that is not really there, illuminates us in a way that makes us forget our self entirely. There is just sun and sunset or perhaps nothing at all to speak of.

The point is, for our spiritual purposes, that there is no hierarchy in this totally connected world. Instead, in every point and at every point, the entire domain of freedom is existent. We don't have to have left the world of subject and object to find God: that is what "God" is for, to bring divine freedom to us as separate beings. We don't have to have erased our egos in order to find enlightenment: indeed, true awakening means that there is a place for our ego in the heart of enlightenment.

The second rule—or rather we should call it "the second encouragement"—is to be utterly honest. This means that we speak our prayers (and in this version of prayerfulness, we need to say our prayer aloud, loud enough so that we can hear what we are saying...) revealing all of who we are at the moment. Again, this method can be used with the dualistic path or the nondual path, so-called, because honesty is the bridge that binds the relative and absolute worlds together. Honesty puts us both in the present moment, devoid of ideas about who we think we should be and simultaneously allows us to be all the different "who-s" we are. In other words, honesty as something we are devoted to, breaks the bonds of all conventions and allows us to incarnate in the present moment with the totality of our being.

Can our selfish desires make an appearance in our prayers? Yes. Can our arrogance and demands? Yes. Can our belief that we are already a Buddha or that we will never be a Buddha appear? Yes. When we do this practice in the way I am suggesting, God and His Creations are one; nirvana and samsara are one. When we do this practice as I am suggesting, things happen. This is a dynamic practice that, as you keep praying for one, two or ten minutes, will change things. Thoughts will change, aliveness will present itself no matter what you are feeling at the moment.

What does the approach to prayer sound like? What are its contents? In a sense, the content doesn't matter as much as the *listening to your own prayer* does. When we listen, we hear. When that circuit of *speaking/hearing/listening* is completed, several things happen at once. First, a dynamic of change begins. Even if your prayer is a simple one of supplication, when you are committed to honesty and listen closely to your own heart as you pray, no longer censoring *what is* in favor of some fantasy of *what should be*, the levels of prayer, what you want to say, will change. And as it changes, the heart of prayer, which is presence, will come into being. You will draw close to what you want, but in a way that changes you.

Presence is the act of being all in one place at one time. It is a form of incarnation into your own life, a way of being intimate and alive with yourself no matter what state you are in. Honesty is the supreme way to enter into presence. It does not need special powers that come and go, but only your own connection to your honesty to make its presence known.

The same is true for chanting any sutra or making supplication to the Buddha. When you are honest, all the contradictions in your soul will emerge—and need to emerge. When those opposites are allowed to remain vividly in your body, mind and spirit, change happens and your prayer is answered, not by a distant deity or flash of nondual lightening which can only last for the briefest of moments, but by presence itself, which is the moment of fitting into your own life and into the lives of others.

When we pray from our heart; when we listen to our own prayer and let it feedback to our heart and allow our heart to arise to the new occasion engendered by the new words, we move along the continuum of being, the human continuum, and find that the separate-only self is indeed separate and has never been separate at all. Both at the same time. And further, we find that there is an answer to our soul's longing at every point and not only at the final one.

When we pray in the manner I described, or indeed in any manner that includes honesty as its touchstone, when we make it our own, our yearnings come to the surface along with our pain. There is room for every human part from suffering to exultation, from supplication to hosanna, from calm certainty to the rough waves of doubt. Through this process *we* come to the surface and we hear ourselves and feel ourselves anew. We enter into a dialogue with the *Great Who-Is* and Buddha becomes real and God enters our heart. The relative world and the absolute world, bridged by this act of honesty, unite, show us their unity since they were never apart, and we too feel whole, human, and wholly alive.

ONLY CONNECT

For good or ill, I have always had a very strong ego—in some ways. I say "in some ways" because every front has a back, an equally strong weakness that lives on the other side of its conscious and front-facing self. This dark brother of the strong ego is equally strong in its weakness. "Weakness" here does not mean *without power*. It is just power of different sort. We could say that this potent weakness is another way of looking at the world. It receives the world differently from its strong counterpart and gives itself to the world in its own distinct way. For example, one side might be primarily concerned with presenting the self to the world while the other side might be more concerned with metabolizing the constant sensory output of this world so that it is not overrun. The variations of this dynamic are probably as endless as the creativity that made our world possible.

Because of the particular and personal shape my ego took—its balance between its front and back sides—I have always gravitated toward trying to overcome its vivid presence and the acute awareness I had of its suffering, imperfections and needs. Because of that, paths that emphasized ego-surrender always seemed like the way to go. The only way I could think of getting free of the strong ego's domain was to find a way to believe that it was not really there, that it had no real existence. In a sense, this was an attempt to live out the shadow side of my ego, misunderstanding its weakness as an egoless state. At the same time, however, this created a double-bind for me since I instinctively knew that denying this front-facing ego and trying to live in this imaginary egoless state denied who and what I was, a perfect person with imperfections, an eternally temporary being. A human.

I was not alone in this imaginary quest to become egoless. *Until this day*, paths abound that try to abolish the ego, some gently and some with force. Some paths like to dissolve this ego in love and some in hate or judgement. But there is a tint in the majority of paths that I have encountered of the need to modify the ego into some sort of transparency, leaving out who it is who wants this, in other words, who's ego has this desire to be invisible! In this distortion, the ego is rarely taken in deeply enough on its own terms to allow the type of transformation that is possible when the whole shape of the personal self is explored in utter nonviolence. So, we are left with this subtle judgement against the ego that lingers in the air like a cheap perfume. We are the judge, jury and defendant in this spiritual drama, and the verdict has come down that we are not worthy as we are. Let me be perfectly clear: I am not talking about simply allowing this ego, with its desire to dominate or disappear, to remain as it is. It needs to be *healed*. What I'd like to describe is another way to heal it.

Last week I had a new thought, that the desire to lessen the tyranny of the ego did not have to be abandoned, but that there was a better way to do it rather than seeking to sublimate this ego through a philosophical rejection of its existence. I had never thought about it *in these words before*. Specifically, the hope to lessen the ego was futile since the ego existed omnipresently in either its strong or shadow form. What would not be futile, however, would be to work at *connecting my ego*—or *the* ego—to others. *Connection of the ego as it is* was the condition that would put the ego in the proper balance, since trying to do away with the ego was just an egoic preoccupation in another form, a wolf in sheep's clothing. Connecting, on the other hand, would be a way of directing the ego to a part of its job—of seeing the world clearly—that would heal it. A healing ego is neither strong nor weak but is simply one engaged in a new way, a less "ego-centric way" if you will.

In connection, the ego finds its own and true level. Let's imagine it this way: one of the usual metaphors in spiritual parlance is the image of a web. This bromide is often used to counteract the exclusively individualistic clothing the personal ego wears. The metaphor of *we are all connected* tilts us toward the impersonal and transcendent rather than toward the personal alone. The insubstantiality of the ego—another true aspect of the ego—is emphasized. This is an attempt to heal the ego's one-sided preoccupation with itself, but it differs from this latest insight in that it still comes down solely on the side of reducing the presence of the ego by essentially looking in a different direction. I am, however, suggesting a different way of healing this dilemma.

If I were to imagine how this idea of connection would play out, I would leave the insubstantiality of the ego for the moment and instead see all the vast egos of the world spread out in front of me like flowers in a giant garden. I wouldn't look for anything else to mitigate this powerful mandala of pure *I-am-ness*. This vast space of individual things would contain all sentient and insentient beings. We could say that it would include all of nature and all of existence except for the fact that there is no prior thing called 'nature' or 'existence', except in these things as they are.

Connecting in this way—allowing our ego to connect with all the other egos of creation—would be our *contribution* of the only thing we truly own: our self. In more traditional spiritual parlance, we would try to get beyond this concept of ownership entirely and see that this precious self was not something we created at all, that we didn't own it in any sense whatsoever, that it was gratuitously gifted upon us by an impersonal universe. But here, I am taking the ego at its own word, that it is *some thing* and *somebody*. From that perspective, it is our most precious possession and the act of *connecting to the array of all ego-individuals* is an act of generosity. We could say it is an act of love that connects us to every other being, rock, tree or person that exists as a separate individual being in the great family of being.

This act has additional consequences. To return to the comments I made above about the strong and weak ego, this new connected stance would allow the powerful sensory existence of the world not to overrun the small, separate self. Connected as it now is, this powerful effusion of energy could be modulated and metabolized. It would no longer be a threat. Additionally, the strong part of the ego could be strong and not link this strength to an imperialist need to survive. This deep connection would now highlight the ever-changing impermanence of the world and yet support the existence of the individual and the individual's responsibility to this web of being.

The broken ego cannot do this. It acts out its drama because it creates the drama to act out, a side-effect of not being connected. The reality of the connected ego leans us toward inter-relatedness and the on-going display of the totality of interconnections as the mandala we see when we are able to stand back and see *is-ness* for what it is. The *connected* ego can do that. The connected ego is an ego whose healing continues not only from the subjective, inside position—or we could say the psychological condition— but arises from pure connection and relationship of which the psychological perspective is only a small and particular view. Seeing the territory of the universal ego, its notion of self-hood spread throughout creation, healing its "I am the only one" nature but maintaining its individuality, happens through give and take, deep respect and the breathing of the world itself. The effort to heal the individual self is now, in other words, part of the universal movement within the individual, connected self. It is intertwined with the innate healing nature of the individual self, and its motive force which comes to the fore as we connect.

As we connect and soften in that way, all of the ego's best qualities come to the surface. Non-ego's don't help other egos: egos help egos. From this position, it is not the formlessness of God that helps and protects, but God's own healing ego that does—and must—reach out to help others. This is Amida Buddha in action, this is the Christ. Even in paths that emphasize the impersonal, this is the Buddha's life force that reaches out in all directions. Personal and impersonal become irrelevant.

I understand that the type of connection I am talking about is a somewhat advanced practice and can only be explored as the personal self has been healed enough of its suffering to *have* a self that can be explored. We have to locate the self before we can live the self. But even so, with this idea in the back of the mind of every helper who wants to help their spiritual friends reduce their suffering, and in the mind of everyone who dares to heal themselves and might hope to heal others, I think we can go far.

COMPASSION IS THE
MEANING OF THE WORLD

Jesus' statement that *the poor are always with us* is not primarily a political statement. It is also not a statement about *the poor in spirit* and our altruistic duty to them, in other words, the skillful means we need to employ to help a suffering world.

Jesus was a skilled metaphysician and, in this statement—often misunderstood—we find the essence of the Christic realization about the nature of the world and its deepest meaning. I'd like to give you a nondual perspective on his teachings.

From a divided point of view—which is sometimes useful to have and has its own grace and importance—there is a deity that looks upon this world from a more exalted and perfected condition and offers aid and comfort. This is of course not only useful, but essential.

But we need to go a bit further: Buddha and Christ, to use just two examples, do not exist in a vacuum or in a separate realm, since the very fact of their spiritual accomplishment ties them inextricably to the suffering world. We can look at it in this way: you become a realized being, a Buddha. You have worked with your own suffering for a lifetime and seen, more and more clearly, the suffering of the world. Where do you go? Doesn't this very level of realization tie you ever-more closely to the relative world? Don't you become more connected to this world even as you partake of a larger vision?

Nonduality takes this even one-step further: Buddha exists because we exist. Because there is brokenness—in each of us and in the world—there is healing. In other words, Buddha and Christ are eternally tied to this imperfect, dusty world because the very core of the Christic or Buddhic realization is about perfection and imperfection, suffering and the release from suffering. It is not about some pristine state of mind but is dependent upon the suffering world for its own existence. Perfection and imperfection interpenetrate each other. Both are vital for the existence of the other. Let's rename "healing" itself as Buddha or Christ or the Torah or the Dharma and let's call "brokenness" our human life, we, who know perfection in our bones but are unable to actualize it.

And here is where it gets interesting: My understanding is that our job as imperfect beings is *not* to perfect ourselves but to *realize* ourselves. To "realize" means something very, very simple. *We remember.* That's it. That's all. We remember our imperfections. We are not swamped by them, overcome by them, shamed by them, or made self-hating by them. We realize we have them, every minute. We bind ourselves to them (even as we work psychologically and physically to correct them—that never stops!) and in that moment of realization, of deep acceptance, the other half of existence—the Buddha-principle, the Christ-principle, appears.

These *universal-dimensional syntaxes*, these ongoing activities of light that we have personified as Buddha or Christ, only "realize" themselves as they meet this rolling imperfection we call "our self." It is then that something remarkable happens: neither ourselves alone, small and imperfect, always on a quest, always trying to get better than we are, nor the Buddha or Christ or any other name you might give it, are what wholeness is, in and of itself. Neither of them alone shows us the nature of the world. But *together*, the nature of the world arises newborn. Or better than "newborn," the never-born and never-dying nature of the world fills our consciousness like morning mist off the side of a vast hill that catches the early morning light. That mist is compassion. We might say that "compassion" is the meaning of the world or that this world—as it is—only becomes meaning-filled from the combination of these perspectives.

Please understand that I am not speaking of a feeling that either side alone in this equation might have. For example, an imperfect going-on-being like you or me, might have *empathy*. Empathy is still a dualistic, and personal emotion. There is a *you* and some other and you (or the other) has a feeling of sympathy for the other one. Great. We all need that, but this is somewhat different from compassion.

Or even looked at from the other side: Buddha's vast openness; Christ's vast connection to the Father. Both are amazing but essentially useless to us. They offer an ocean, wet and salty, when what we need in the moment is clear and fresh and in a small glass. It is only when this vastness meets us as beings who have accepted, bound ourselves to the truth of our "*complete partialness*," our own eternally imperfect self, that both disappear (and yet, paradoxically remain); then *compassion*, which does not belong to anyone, Buddha or Christ, man or woman, appears.

Compassion is man-woman-Christ-in-action. Compassion is Buddha-in-action. Compassion is vast-mountain consciousness in the morning mist surrounding a tiny seedling. Compassion is not personal. You don't own compassion; compassion owns you. It is in the field of compassion that our lives change. It is within this condition that great things and small things can be done. This is why we have "Jesus" as well as "Christ," and "Gautama Shakyamuni" in addition to "Buddha."

In our ignorance, we always go for one half of the equation. If we are put upon by our heritage or karma, our neuroses, our *least parts*, we gravitate toward thinking of ourselves as the smallest, most injured beings. If we see ourselves in this way, we naturally—but incorrectly—see the other half of the equation as that perfected, personal being who will save us. We then quest after them and do not see that they quest after us.

The streams of being that Buddha and Christ are don't save us because they take something away from us. Instead, the type of salvation that comes from connecting to these *being-nesses* comes because it invariably asks us to return to true relationship with who we are, broken beings who also know wholeness and are guided by it even as we can never reach it.

It is then that we smell the fragrance of the compassion that is at the root of the world, that arises for us human–going-on-beings as the left and right are held together. It is then we meet the real Buddha; the real Christ, the one who was always here and who we've always embodied under our layers of fear and misconception. There he is. There she is. There we are. And the world goes on.

AGAINST MY INSISTENCE ON NONDUALITY

It has occurred to me, after a lifetime of studying the perspective of nonduality, that this precious gift, which has meant so much to me, must be carefully laid down to rest.

As it turns out, many of the elements I had associated with a nondual perspective, such as the co-arising of subject and object, of this and that, of the personal self and the impersonal self, of the continuity and density, began to feel less and less important. I had in many ways, depended upon this level of consciousness because—I see now—it lowered the level of conflict within me and my perception of the world, and thus, allowed me to exist and teach in it with less strain and judgement and more spaciousness. That said, I began to notice a soft glow of nondual consciousness, of some subtle work I had to do on a moment-by-moment basis in order to maintain this awareness. Whether that was because this awareness was not deeply settled enough in my soul or for some other, unknown reason, I began to both be aware of this level of effort and the co-arising of my decision to end this type of relationship. It had all at once begun to feel inauthentic, effort-filled and out of touch with something I needed to return to.

A new level of "non-awareness" needed to take its place. I say "non-awareness" because I was looking for something that was so direct, so plain that it needed no explanatory intervals or philosophical understanding in order to be touched. It was a tactile need, uncomplicated and direct. I wanted to touch something that this glow seemed to be in the way of. Whether that thing was going to be brighter or darker did not enter into my calculations. There was no longer room for me at that particular inn.

Why was this forgetting necessary? By that I mean, did I have to forget in some manner the truth of the co-arising unity in order to feel this ordinary freedom and ordinary joy? I am contemplating saying "yes." At least for me, and more accurately, at least for me at this moment, this was necessary and might be for at least a period of time.

Recently, I had a session with someone who had a series of experiences which, while of great fulfilment for her, were still somehow dual: there was still "someone" or "something" standing apart from the experiencer who was the causative factor in all this freedom coming to fruition. As I noted this in my notes and wondered about—and then rejected—leading this person to a more nondual, co-arising view, I also put down this note: "This person's dualistic view may also be a true view!" What I felt in that moment was that anything but what this person was feeling was extraneous. In this particular case, the end result of this person's experience was an abundance of tenderness, compassion and love. The nondual view per se was something extra, a "thing" not needed in the ultimate flow of the feelings and insights that flowed from this experience for this person. It was true that my experience of understanding and living the nondual view had brought me to the lip of tenderness, that without understanding the nature of a co-arising universe, I would never have seen the scintillation of the world at all. Now, however, all that stood in my way was the very light I had worked so hard to find.

On a helping basis in this session, I decided to take things as they were, not with some hidden consciousness within me of some technical virtuosity wherein I held back some deeper truth to allow this "relative" truth to settle into this person's consciousness. Instead, I radically abandoned my thought of there being anything else that was "deeper," since where this person had arrived was where I had arrived through my own devotion to the nondual. The nondual had "cast me out" on this farther shore—if it was a farther shore! In fact, I no longer cared whether it was farther or closer, a shore or a sea. It was only where I was and where

I was going. I knew somatically at that point something that perhaps other spiritual devotees might have known from the beginning, which was that nonduality, if it is to be embodied and real and not an especially refined and special state, must lead back to creation itself, with its messy "nothingness," with its muddy light sometimes and its bright light sometimes. That "higher" must always have "lower" compassionately nested within it and that my job was to breathe it all in. All special states needed to cease— or not cease. They were irrelevant in the face of the larger truth, which was that everything we do can and should be in the service of love.

Love must bring us back to the particular. We love something and someone. We love the entire picture. We cry for the entire picture. Creation is seen as something wonderful and terrible and not something that only reveals its truest essence to the high and mighty. And, after all, we must see the infinite as the abode of the particular and the open hands and heart that absolves all of creation of the idea of "sin," of higher and lower. And yes, of course, there is still higher and lower and "sin" and right and wrong. The point is: there is room for all without condescension and without holding something in abeyance because it is not yet "the highest truth." Letting go of all that seemed to me to be a higher truth; nonduality—at least in the way I had unknowingly held it in my heart—was a bridle on a horse that simply wanted to graze in the spring grass. I didn't want this bridle on my soul. I wanted to fully appreciate this person as they were, beautifully ensconced in the particulars of creation in this world of duality, tender in time, love in the length and width of a human life.

I freely admit my ignorance and lack of attainment in this area. It feels freeing to do so. It feels even more wonderful to give up the thought of any spiritual attainment and instead yoke myself to the job of simply being a better person, that knowing that my life will end, focusing my job on making this span, this time, this finite bit of the universe's history, a loving one.

I understood that the teacher helps by being love and not by loving. Loving always contains its opposite and can, in a way, hold within it the threat of desolation and exile in those moments you cannot muster or master the connection with love. In other words, there is always the possibility of "something else." But being love on the other hand, was an entirely different animal. It was an animal fully aware of flesh and blood, fully ready to sit with anyone and discourse and drink tea and listen and learn and teach and lead—all at the same time. It has—as much as possible given the limits of our knowledge and ability, at least in my case—the possibility of giving up territory, giving up a border wall against the infinite in its multiplicity, so that reality rushes in and a bow in every direction is the only correct answer to the vagaries of human life, a bow even to my own ineptitude and failure to always embody the love I so clearly see.

Please understand: this little note to eternity is not about nonduality per se. It is about my limited understanding and how those small notions kept me from this plainer view. I know that I will continue to teach the nondual view since it leads inextricably to this here and now. But I won't live in its elevated castle, a castle I put it in, in my ignorance. In the future, I hope I will continue to see it as a simple tool that can lead people back to this boisterous, dangerous and beautiful world, with its valleys of truth and its crevices of evil. It did that for me.

ABOUT THE JASON SHULMAN LIBRARY

Over the past forty years of teaching, Jason Shulman has worked to reconcile the deistic or relative paths of liberation with the consciousness of Buddhism and other non-theistic paths to create a truly nondual path of healing that does not exclude any aspect of reality. His work emphasizes the healing of the personal ego and its rightful place in any path that seeks liberation from ignorance and the awakening of compassion. His work also seeks to bring the truly human world, with its imperfections, into alignment with the realization of transcendent awareness. More about the Library and Jason's work and outreach can be found at the Foundation for Nonduality website: www.nonduality.us.com

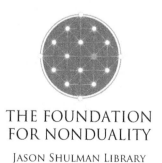

THE FOUNDATION
FOR NONDUALITY
JASON SHULMAN LIBRARY

Made in the USA
Coppell, TX
15 January 2021